DYNAMIC STOCK OPTION TRADING

Dynamic Stock Option Trading

JOSEPH T. STEWART, Jr.

A Ronald Press Publication

JOHN WILEY & SONS, New York • Chichester • Brisbane • Toronto • Singapore

Library of Congress Cataloging in Publication Data:

Stewart, Joseph T. Jr.   1931–
  Dynamic stock option trading.

  "A Ronald Press publication."
  Includes index.
  1. Put and call transactions. I. Title.

HG6042.S8   332.64′25   80–25957
ISBN 0–471–08670–3

Printed in the United States of America

10 9 8 7 6 5 4

To

Carolyn, Thomas, and Allison

Preface

This book is for those of you who are interested in the trading of listed stock options, as I am, and who have been striving, as I have been striving, to find a profitable way in which to participate in this dynamic expanding part of the equity market.

Certainly there has been no lack of books published in the past few years on both technical and fundamental approaches to investing and trading in the stock market. In addition, there have been many texts written on trading stock options since the inception of active options markets such as the Chicago Board of Options Exchange, where options were first actively traded in 1973.

To date, however, I have not read such a book for the layman who wants to do his own trading, but feels at a disadvantage because his time is limited, he doesn't have a computer for analysis or the technique to utilize one, and he doesn't have constant access to a market quote machine.

I feel that through my learning experiences (both good and bad) and actual practice and implementation I have succeeded in putting together just such a system.

Because the end product of my effort evolved out of the work and experiences of others, shared with me through their books, articles, and lectures, I feel I should in turn share what *I* have learned, and that I can make a contribution to the art of marketing timing, the selection of stocks for option trading, and, my basic objective, profitable trading in call and put options.

I have combined some ideas from previously published materials, added some ideas of my own, and developed a checkpoint system for short-term timing of trades that is a new and powerful combination. Credit is given throughout the book to the authors whose work I have used. I am greatly indebted to them.

Once I started to write the text, I found it easy—I was simply organizing and putting into words what I had learned and practiced over the past five years. The discipline required to put the material in a logical order that a reader could follow became a personal advantage to me. My work on the book started to improve my *own* performance, since writing about its techniques and guidelines became a constant reminder that I must rigidly follow my own trading rules and methods if I am to convince others of their value.

Others have commented that once a system is published its usefulness and effectiveness are destroyed as it becomes a popular trading method. I do not believe this is true.

First, the market is large and my system concentrates on major high-priced stocks with large capitalizations.

Second, my system involves the *option,* and not the underlying stock, which moves according to the supply and demand *for the stock itself,* so followers of any option trading method do not usually affect the stock price. Conceivably the method could be used for trading the underlying stocks as well, but not as profitably since there is greater leverage in option movement.

Third, relatively few traders will have the persistence and discipline to use *any* particular system to the extent that it causes distortion in the movement of options or their underlying stocks.

I hope this book will offer some useful ideas and guidelines, and perhaps give the reader a different perspective on option trading. I further hope that the step-by-step guidance through the aspects of technical analysis which has proved of so much value to me will lead the reader along the path to a better understanding of market dynamics.

The Stewart System is as simple and as time-saving as I have been able to make it. It has worked well for me. I leave it to you, the reader, to decide for yourself what value this book has for you. If nothing else, it should give you some powerful tools to use in improving your timing and selection of stocks—whether for conservative investing or short-term option trading.

I would like to mention that I hope the women reading this book will not take me to task for my use of masculine pronouns. He/she, person, and so forth, sound stilted to me, and therefore I choose to stick with "he," which I intend to be read for either gender.

JOSEPH T. STEWART, JR.

Houston, Texas
January 1981

Acknowledgments

I wish to thank the many people who helped increase my understanding of the market through study and exchange of their ideas. Additional recognition is given throughout the book to those few authors whose works made such an impact on me with their original thinking and provided me with the basis for my combination of methods.

I wish to thank Carla Jennings, who edited the original manuscript and made many helpful suggestions and additions, which added both clarity and content. She also drew the diagrams and constructed the final stock charts for printing.

Special appreciation goes to my secretary, Carole Bossley, who typed, and retyped, the manuscript and assembled it for submission to the publisher.

But, most of all, I wish to thank my understanding wife, Carolyn, for her enduring patience with me and her good-natured acceptance of the endless hours spent on my charts and books—in the evenings, on the weekends, and during vacations. Her help in producing this book is intangible, but the most important of all.

J. T. S.

Contents

Figures

DYNAMIC STOCK
OPTION TRADING

PART ONE

How I Came to Develop My System for Option Trading

The stock market has always been one of my greatest interests and, for the last several years, I have had the ambition to become a successful trader, searching for the elements that would provide a systematic approach and a logical way to make trading decisions. Like most people who study the market in depth, my thinking, methods, and approach have changed greatly over this period of time.

Because I am an engineer by profession, I don't like to deal with intangibles if I can help it. Therefore, early in my quest for a trading system that was right for me, I decided my primary approach must be based on technical analysis. I wanted to be able to visualize my trades, measure my results, see clear-cut signals. I wanted to set goals, achieve them, and establish a discipline that would keep me out of trouble.

I devoted many hours of my free time to the search. I read the new books that were published and followed some of the ideas they put forth. I attended costly seminars and lectures. Gradually, I narrowed down my area of interest to short-term option trading, with an approach based on technical analysis. I became convinced that here was the vehicle for making the greatest return with the least amount of capital (i.e., with limited risk) in the shortest possible time.

SHORT-TERM OPTION TRADING IS SPECULATION

A person who engages in short-term option trading is a *speculator*. A speculator is willing to take a great deal more risk than an investor is, in the hope of building substantial profits in a shorter period of time. He must have available an amount of capital that he can afford to lose.

1

He does not speculate with money needed for necessities. He doesn't use all of his savings or his retirement funds for speculation. His speculating money should be set aside for this purpose. Such is the nature of speculation.

Having reached the decision that I wanted to try my hand at speculating (as opposed to investing), I decided I had better take a closer look at myself and my own personality to decide whether I had the emotional make-up to be a short-term trader. I made a list of some of the character traits I believed the successful short-term trader must have. I believe he

- Craves action.
- Keeps up to date on the market and the economy.
- Is constantly alert to new opportunities.
- Wants to know where he stands at all times.
- Wants to be able to measure the elements in his decision making, to better predict results.
- Wants to make his own decisions.
- Is able to decide quickly and definitely.
- Strives to be correct in his decisions.
- Develops short-term goals, confident these will lead to greater long-term success.
- Is self-critical and honest with himself.
- Admits his mistakes and learns from them.
- Is eager to continue to learn through study and experience.
- Does not become discouraged easily or quit after a setback.
- Is willing to work hard for success.

My conclusion was that my personality fit the role of the short-term option trader. The next step was to learn how to trade profitably in the fast-moving options market.

Since the trading of options carries the risk of losing all of your capital if you make a mistake, I concentrated my study on correct timing and the identification of profitable trading situations, and getting out quickly when I was wrong. These seemed to be the key factors to successful short-term option trading.

I further limited my area of specialization to only the *buying and selling of call and put option contracts,* reasoning that a simple, direct approach would keep my thoughts uncluttered, be easier to keep up with on a part-time basis, and fit a busy life style. I purposely excluded from my plan (as I have from this book) all of the complicated hedging techniques, the sophisticated strategies like spreads, straddles, butterflies, being long and short at the same time, naked and covered writing of options, and so forth, that are so confusing to understand, of limited profit potential, and costly to work with.

I became convinced that correct timing is *the one key ingredient* for success in trading options, especially since stock options are a wasting asset that decay with time because of their short life. They must be considered in this light as the type of speculative trading vehicle they are. As one old market maxim states, "Don't just tell me *what* to buy, tell me *when* to buy it." That is what this book and the Stewart System will try to show the serious option trader—how to improve your timing and selection.

ONE

What Is the Stewart System?

To attempt to describe the Stewart System in a few sentences is a difficult task, but I will try to put it "in a nutshell" so you can get an idea of the scope of the material to be covered in this book. Essentially, the Stewart System is a blend of three basic disciplines, the purpose of which is to help the average person who wants to speculate in the options market to improve his results.

PSYCHOLOGY

A successful trader must really understand market psychology. He knows that whatever the insiders and the smart money are thinking is usually just the opposite of what the public is thinking. He is well informed on the market, the economy, and the political climate; he keeps up to date with events on a day-to-day basis because market psychology can reverse in a second.

TECHNICAL ANALYSIS

In order to know what is really happening in the market and in an individual stock one should learn to use market indicators and technical analysis. Utilizing these skills allows one to spot signals that indicate changes in market conditions, gives one buy and sell signals that enhance trading results, and points out unusual opportunities before the crowd becomes aware of them. These skills can also provide confirmation that one's decisions are correct.

MECHANICAL TRADING METHODS

The Stewart System tries to *anticipate* future action, to be ready to move quickly ahead of the crowd, but *does not take action* unless a clear signal is given (preferably with additional *confirmation*). It is a system for taking action on buy and sell signals, but it strives to integrate market psychology, good judgment, confirmation from as many sources as possible—and then rigidly follows the mechanical trading rules. Following the trading rules helps you to take full advantage of profitable opportunities and—just as important—helps to get you out of a bad situation with minimum loss when you are wrong.

To sum up, my system is a blend of the best techniques of technical analysis (for both market timing and timing in individual stocks) that I have been able to find for the layman to work with, together with a knowledge of market psychology and mechanical trading methods to aid the decision-making process. In essence, the system says, "always follow the market, learn to anticipate what the market is likely to do next based on psychology and established cyclic patterns, and then wait for confirmation that you are right."

The Stewart System advocates following closely the action of some individual stocks (representative of various industries) on a daily basis. These stocks should be selected for special characteristics—past cyclic patterns that are likely to continue, price action boundaries you can measure and project, ones with individual characteristics that you will come to know so well with your day-to-day charting that you can easily recognize their buy and sell signals when they occur.

The system stresses not taking action in the option market unless you have all the right elements going for you—the right psychology, the right market timing, and a clear buy or sell signal—with confirmation that you are right. Even then, there is no guarantee of success—technical analysis is not an exact science, but more of an art. Just as no two artists paint the same subject in the same way, and no two musicians interpret a piece of music in exactly the same way, so technical analysis is subject to personal interpretation. Some people will be more skilled at it than others; some will see things that others are not even aware of; and some will bring to it an intuitive sense while others will try to interpret it literally and mechanically. Perhaps this is why some very important and successful market analysts and financial advisors discount the usefulness of technical analysis, while at the other extreme there are those who follow slavishly the pronouncements of a particular technical analyst in what amounts to a cult following. I advocate listening to what the better ones have to say—but I believe you should do your *own* technical work, do your *own* thinking, and make your *own* decisions.

I have presented in this book the methods I have been working with. They are working well for me—maybe they can be of use to you. How you use the material, how you interpret it, whether you can trade options successfully using my methods will depend on you: how hard you work at it, how you interpret what you learn from it, how your own style and personality interact to create your own personal system.

Ideally, my system, your system, or any system for that matter, in order to be current, effective, and up to date, should be able to incorporate changes as they become necessary. Assimilate new ideas, try a new indicator, improve an old one if a new set of market statistics becomes available. Be on the lookout for new techniques. Discard out-of-date material and methods when they cease to be useful. Any system can be improved upon!

TWO

Psychology in the Stock Market

The psychology of the stock market may be described as the existing attitude of people toward the market. In other words it is the "crowd" of people buying or selling every day that causes price movement and direction. It has been said that the market at any one time reflects the total knowledge, hopes, dreams, and fears of those individuals participating. And yet each person has his own emotional makeup that influences his actions, which, in turn, are influenced externally by the overall market movement. If a person could isolate himself from crowd psychology he would *not* necessarily make the same decisions.

Major swings in the market can be caused by crowd behavior. For example, when fundamental business and economic conditions are best, the market can make a major top as the majority of eager and enthusiastic buyers expects even higher prices. At the other end of the spectrum, crowd behavior can cause the majority to sell stock at low prices when the economic news is worst. Mass movement by the crowd greatly influences each of us as individuals, and causes our emotions to take over our judgment during these extreme conditions, as we "join the crowd." At times, this emotional buying and selling can cause the market, or an individual stock, to move up or down a much greater distance than we would normally expect, or dream, is possible. A good example of crowd behavior is the bidding up of a "fad" or "popular" segment of the stock market beyond any reasonable near-term or long-term value. These situations always top, then move down dramatically in price as the enthusiasm wanes, and the latest buyers can only sell at a loss. Obviously at these tops an opinion completely contrary to the crowd would have been the correct one.

Some recent examples of this phenomenon, which you may remember, were the extreme run-up in the gambling stocks in 1978–1979, the wild speculation in gold and silver, and in *any* company that had natural resources ("assets in the ground") in early 1980. Another example of crowd psychology at work is the way domestic oil stocks take off every time the OPEC countries raise the price of their oil, or threaten to cut off supplies. Rising oil prices cause a cutback in fuel use and a "glut" develops. Oil stocks drop again. Whenever the Mideast or other world trouble spot heats up, fear of war sends aerospace and government contract related stocks soaring. As fears cool down, these stocks drop in price.

A new concept or marketing idea sometimes catches the public fancy and runs related stocks to ridiculous highs. Remember the Wankel engine? CB radios? Remember how one motion picture, *Star Wars,* ran up the stock of the movie company that produced it? While we shouldn't take a concept or idea too seriously, we certainly should profit by understanding the crowd psychology behind it; and by riding the moves with the rest of the crowd (providing we don't get carried away and become hypnotized) we can take our profits early and let the others stampede over the cliff!

When an individual does not have a clear idea of what is going on in the market and just tries to hang on, doing what the crowd seems to be doing, following the advice of others, and getting wiped out time after time, he may begin to think that the market exists only to separate him from his money. This will certainly be true if he follows the majority since the majority does not make a net gain over a long period of time. The expression that "the market will do whatever it can to confuse the greatest number of investors," is probably true. When people are concerned about inflation, deflation, their current and future economic condition, politics, and world affairs, these things will add to their confusion in their outlook on the stock market. A person can obtain as many conflicting opinions and ideas as he wants to read about the market, and this further adds to his confusion.

Regardless of our modern way of living with all the conveniences we enjoy, our basic emotional makeup and behavior probably have not changed much since the beginning of time. The strongest emotion, fear, is one of the main forces we must learn to control in our stock market activity. Excitability or excess enthusiasm can distort our good judgment at other times. We must learn to control these feelings in order to make correct, unemotional market decisions.

Since all of us have the same basic emotions, how do we learn to keep them in check and use them to improve rather than penalize our performance in the market?

The only method I have ever found that helps to overcome emotional decision making is through the use of technical indicators that allow me to judge market conditions for myself, rather than just taking someone else's opinion or guessing about what is going on. Regardless of what is written or said about stocks or the market, you should only be interested in what people are *actually doing* in the market, which translates into *supply and demand,* and therefore price. You will find that I often refer to this concept because it is really the basis of my trading system.

When you learn to use the skills of technical analysis you will start making more objective decisions in your stock market trading and you will be no longer influenced by the psychology of the crowd.

THREE

My Personal Approach to the Stock Market

Professional financial advisors who give opinions and advice on the market and stocks usually base their work on fundamental analysis or technical analysis (or a combination of the two). Those who adhere rigidly to one philosophy or the other will continue to debate the merits of each approach for as long as there are markets to trade in.

THE FUNDAMENTAL APPROACH IS CONCERNED WITH FACTS AND PROJECTIONS

Annual reports, quarterly earning reports, earnings projections, economic news, industry conditions, government reports, ad infinitum gleaned from all the published (and unpublished) material that is available to the analyst, are the tools the fundamentalist works with. He must read, analyze, weigh, form an opinion, make a projection, and compare his projections with the projections of other analysts. In spite of the fact that almost everything there is to know about the stock, the industry, or the economy is also available to everyone else (company insiders, who may know more, are prohibited by law from talking), few analysts agree in their projections. How can an individual who wants to make his own decisions hope to cope with all this conflicting input?

After studying the fundamental factors for a company and then looking at a chart of the stock's price action, you will usually find that fundamentals are out of time synchronization with the stock price action. You

13

may be baffled to see a stock top out and drop rapidly in price just as a good earnings report is released. Or sometimes, even when the earnings peak seems to have been reached, the stock will not top out for several months.

Sometimes the stock price action may precede a fundamental change in a company's fortune by many months—long before the change in earnings trend becomes apparent, signaling whether it is to be up or down. Also, we can be fundamentally right in our earnings projection only to have a stock perform in just the opposite manner. The psychology of the market crowd in its enthusiasm and greed, or its fear and depression, may also greatly influence the stock price even though the sales and earnings performance are right on target. A takeover bid can completely throw off any fundamental projections. An unfounded rumor can play havoc with a stock's price.

Fundamental factors *are* important—a person who involves himself in the market *must* be aware of and take into consideration important fundamental factors. No one will dispute that such things as rising or falling interest rates, the business cycle with its inflation, recession, and recovery phases, the machinations of the Federal Reserve Board, trade deficits, foreign currency translations, the money supply, the presidential political term, and so on, all have a profound impact on the market as a whole and individual stocks in particular.

I believe the strictly fundamental approach is most successful for the *long-term* investor. If he buys a stock at the bottom of its long-term trading range and patiently holds it (possibly for years) and then sells it when it returns to the upper limits of its long-term trading range, he can be very successful.

But what about the person who wants some profit *now?* The person who does not want to tie up his capital for the long term? The person who wants to speculate and make his money grow more rapidly through compounding? Short-term trading on a fundamental basis is just not practical. Most of the time the fundamental projections made about a stock or industry have long been discounted in the marketplace before the actual earnings are released. The expectations are past history in terms of stock price action. While the fundamentalist is looking at growth rates, outlook for sales and earnings, relationship to other stocks in the same industry, trends and forecasts in the economy, estimated dividend payout, and so forth, the technical analyst is looking at entirely different things.

WHY TECHNICAL ANALYSIS BEATS FUNDAMENTAL ANALYSIS FOR TRADING OPTIONS

The technician, unlike the fundamentalist, looks at chart action and history, support zones, resistance zones, relative strength in relation to the market, volume, moving averages, cycles, and other physical measurements that are interpreted from past action. His approach is, "Don't confuse me with the facts about the company in question; show me what the stock trading action is, and I'll make my decision."

Both camps have their place and both are successful in their predictions some of the time, or the two methods would not continually be followed by their advocates. Of course, throwing darts at the stock tables also has been successful some of the time!

An individual approach might be fundamental or technical, or a combination of both. After several years of studying and trading in the market, I chose to follow the technical approach as opposed to the fundamental. Like everyone else, I appreciate a good fundamental story on an earnings projection, merger, new product, and so forth, but I always analyze the chart action and refer to other market-timing indicators before taking a position. These other factors must fall into place or a "special situation" has a good chance of sandbagging me. This has happened to me too many times.

YOU CAN'T HIDE SUPPLY AND DEMAND

The only thing that causes stock prices to change is *supply and demand,* or selling pressure versus buying pressure. This occurs every day that stocks are traded on the exchange. Technical measurements and observations of chart phenomena can be used to measure supply and demand as these stocks are being traded, and these are the only tools I know of that will improve the odds in predicting short-term trading movements.

Supply and demand cannot be hidden, if we know what to look for on a chart. The range of the day's price action (from high to low, from open to close, from yesterday's close to today's open), together with the ebb and flow of the volume of shares that are traded during the day, all give us a true picture of what is happening to the supply and demand of a stock.

Big price moves on very low volume are always suspicious, short-lived, and dangerous to trade. But big price moves accompanied by large or massive volume really indicate something is happening!

YOU MUST CONSIDER VOLUME

Volume is the engine that moves stocks and the market in general. The *amount* of supply and demand in a stock is measured by the volume of trading. An accurate measurement of the effect of the day's trading volume on the supply/demand picture is another important tool I use for making trading decisions. More about this tool, and how I use it, is presented later in this book.

TIMING: THE MOST IMPORTANT ELEMENT

Timing is the most important element in buying or selling any stock or option. From my own experience (and I think this would be mirrored in the experiences of most people who attempt to speculate in stocks or options) timing is the toughest and most important element to identify. If our timing technique can be consistently improved, our success will be compounded many times over in a period of active trading.

DON'T FOLLOW THE HERD—
WATCH ACCUMULATION/DISTRIBUTION

The biggest hurdle in the struggle to improve our timing is resisting the "follow-the-herd" instinct. We are all inclined to be enthusiastic along with everyone else. We tend to be pessimistic at the same time the majority feels that way. We must separate ourselves from this crowd, and coolly, analytically, base our decisions on measurable technical indications. This idea is the basis for the material presented in this book.

We must ask the question, what can we do to buy low and sell high? Most of the time the answer is we must do exactly the opposite of what our emotions tell us to do. We must have the courage to buy stocks when they are the least popular—after a long drop, when they seem to be in a sideways pattern of base building; when no one else seems interested in them; when there has been only bad news for months, or no news at all. This is when we detect *accumulation* beginning. The smart money is starting to accumulate the stock in anticipation of its moving up. This may not be apparent to the general public for quite some time, but we have to learn to detect it early. (More about how to do this in later chapters.)

Conversely, we must be able to sell promptly when everyone else is enthusiastic. Earnings reports are great; a new product has been announced; brokers are touting the stock; people are discussing its prospects at cocktail parties. Our best friend suggests we buy some more—it is going to go through the roof! This is the phase we will be able to identify as the beginning of *distribution*. Distribution is the phase when the smart money is unloading its long positions to the public and establishing short sales for the coming downtrend.

This kind of thinking is 180 degrees away from what most everyone else is thinking. We might say it is the *contrary opinion* that gets results in the stock market. Our emotions are the biggest single block that prevent us from doing the right thing at the right time. The only way I know to overcome this is to get a mechanical timing system that takes as much of the emotion out of the decision-making process as possible.

The Stewart System for option trading follows the technical rules that are explained further in the text. The main feature of the system is that it is technical and mechanical in nature and really does not need any fundamental explanation to predict price changes.

THE TWO TO FIVE PERCENT WHO ARE SUCCESSFUL TRADERS: HOW CAN WE JOIN THE CLUB?

I have often heard the statement that perhaps 2–5 percent of the people who actively trade stocks in the market actually make a net profit from their transactions. From my observations, I believe this is true. I have studied and worked hard to try to move into this two to five percent. Obviously, this small group consists of the disciplined and knowledgeable who can take the right action at the right time. It is not a question of luck, but it is a question of consistently applying a systematic approach, and one that is not followed by the majority. It stands to reason that those who have the most knowledge of timing and selection, and can take action contrary to the crowd, are going to be among those few who can win in the stock market or stock option game.

SOME PERSONAL PHILOSOPHICAL OBSERVATIONS

I look upon the market as a giant arena in which many people wish to play the game for many different reasons. Perhaps some are on an ego trip and like to talk about the fact that they are trading in the market. These people normally talk about their successes, but seldom admit their wrong decisions and the number of big baths they periodically take by wrong actions. I also think we should be completely honest with ourselves and admit our mistakes as well as our successes, especially if we want to discuss our trading results with anyone else.

I think most of us secretly would like to be successful speculators in life and really make some money the smart way, if we could only figure out how to do it. Most people would not admit this, although they play bingo or gamble in Las Vegas with the hope of winning big against fixed odds. It is a fact, however, that successful stock or stock option traders *do not* trade against fixed odds or a stacked deck. That is the difference between gambling and speculation.

Certainly, trading in the market is interesting and exciting. However, we should not do it just for exhilaration, but should take a hardheaded, analytical approach if we plan to increase our capital and enjoy the benefits of this increase. I believe also we should use some of our market gains to increase our standard of living and spend some of the proceeds as we make them. This may mean getting out of debt, buying things we want that we normally could not afford, or taking a much needed vacation. If we do this from time to time, the market can never completely separate us from the gains we have won, and it will ensure some personal satisfaction and reward along the way.

FOUR

How Options Provide Outstanding Profit Opportunities for the Short-Term Trader

I assume the reader has an understanding of stock option terms and a familiarity with the option market, but if not, a discussion of a few definitions will be helpful as a starting reference. We are only going to discuss some of the basics for open call or put positions, leaving more complicated trading strategies to others. If you want to go into greater detail, some helpful books are listed at the end of this chapter.

CALLS

A "call" option is a contract that entitles the buyer to *buy* shares of stock (usually 100 shares) at a specific striking price at any time during the period that the option is in force. In most cases, the buyer of a call purchases it from the holder or owner of the underlying stock. The proceeds that do not go for brokerage commissions accrue to the seller (or writer) of the call. The call writer wants to gain income from selling calls against the stock that he owns (while continuing to hold the stock) and he also gets some downside protection against loss if the stock price drops during the time the option is in force. (His stock position is protected by the amount he receives as a premium for writing the call.)

There are also writers of call options who do not *own* the underlying stock. Uncovered writers, (or "naked" writers as they are sometimes referred to) are speculating that the stock will go down and the option will expire worthless, and they will get to keep the premium they received. If the stock goes up instead, the option may be exercised, forcing the uncovered writer to purchase the stock at the current market price for delivery to the call buyer who is exercising the call. An uncovered writer must put up sufficient money with his broker to cover a purchase of the stock, should the option be exercised. (There are other ramifications and hedging techniques related to uncovered writing of options, but since writing options lies outside the scope of this book, I simply refer you to the books listed at the end of this chapter, should you desire more information on the subject.)

The call buyer on the other hand wants the stock to rise in price so that he can either exercise the call and buy the stock at the striking price or sell the call to another buyer for a higher price. In most cases call options are sold to close the position, rather than to purchase or take delivery of the stock at the stipulated striking price.

A call option on 100 shares of stock gives you control of the shares for a limited time at a fixed price without receiving any dividends on the stock. The stock price normally discounts the amount of the dividend that will be paid, and the price of the option premium usually reflects the ex-dividend stock price over the short term.

By a wide margin, most option buyers are outright speculators. Investors, on the other hand, are those who own large positions in stocks and frequently sell (or write) calls against these positions to gain income from their stock holdings, or to partially protect their holdings from downside risk. However, they do risk that the stock will rise in value by an amount greater than the striking price and that the stock may then be called away or bought from them by the option buyer who has the right to buy at that striking price. This may occur at any time during the period the option is in force, and the owner of the stock must deliver the stock to the option buyer through the Option Clearing Corporation if the contract is exercised. The stock owner keeps the option premium that he receives from the call buyer, but he forfeits all gain in the stock above the striking price at which he wrote the call.

CLOSING A CALL POSITION

If you are the *buyer* of the call option, and the expiration date is at hand, only three things can occur:

1. The call can be exercised and you can purchase the stock from the call writer at the striking price.
2. The call option can be sold to close the position.
3. The option can expire worthless if the stock is below the striking price at expiration (or if you neglect to close the position before it expires).

If you are the *writer* of the call option, and the expiration date is at hand, the following can occur:

1. The option may be exercised, and you will have to sell your stock to the call buyer at the striking price (this is likely to happen if the stock price is considerably above the striking price).
2. You can close the position by *buying* a call (this cancels your obligation to surrender your stock) which may cost you more than you received for the call that you wrote, or may actually cost much less, if the price rise has not been substantial. A person who wants to keep his stock position would choose this alternative.
3. If the stock is at striking price or below, you do not need to do anything, because the worthless call will not be exercised. You can keep your stock and the option premium you received.

It is confusing to the person unfamiliar with options that explanations are usually given in terms of what will happen at the expiration of the contract. It should be emphasized that this is not what the short-term option trader is interested in. He is concerned with what will happen to the option during its contract life—three weeks, three months, six months, nine months, or whatever—and not what happens at expiration. One of the basic premises of this book is that the short-term option trader *does not hold his contracts until expiration, nor does he plan to exercise them.* He merely wants to make a profit on the fluctuations in option price which occur as the underlying stock moves up and down in price within its short-term trading range.

HOW OPTION PRICES FLUCTUATE

To understand what happens when option prices fluctuate during the life of the contract, it is necessary to understand the terms "intrinsic value" and "time premium," and how they affect option price.

The price of an option has two components—intrinsic value and time premium. The time (or speculative) premium is the price that a buyer is willing to pay for the privilege of buying the stock (should he wish to do so) at the striking price during the life of the option. The intrinsic value of an option only applies when the option is "in-the-money" or above the striking price. For example, if a stock is trading at $52 and there is a $50 call available, the intrinsic value of the call will be $2. If the option is trading at $3½, $2 of that represents intrinsic value and $1½ represents the time premium.

Should the stock be trading *below* the striking price of the option, the option is said to be "out-of-the-money." The only value an out-of-the-money option has is the amount of time premium speculators are willing to pay for the gamble that the price of the stock will rise. Spectacular gains can be made this way, but one must keep in mind that if the stock remains at or below the striking price, the option will have no intrinsic value but only time premium value, which will disappear as time passes. This is why I prefer to work with in-the-money options which have intrinsic value. They give you a chance to get some of your money back should the position not develop as you anticipate.

The longer the term of the option, the greater the dollar amount of time premium the option will have. However, a better measure of time premium is the *percent of time premium per month of time left in the contract*. This is usually greatest in those options that have one to three months left before expiration. Speculation and trading volume increase as the time period shortens and the open interest increases. (The open interest is the total number of contracts actually in existence at a given time.) This means that six and nine month options, even though higher priced, do not have a greater percentage of time premium per month of life remaining than one and three month options. Percent of time premium per month can be extremely high for options of popular, volatile stocks that are trading near the striking price and are close to expiration date because the options are highly leveraged and speculation in these options is at its highest level during this time.

But this is not the whole story. The call option will fluctuate in price during the life of the contract just as the price of the underlying stock will fluctuate. In addition, the time premium portion of the contract will change also. If the stock does not go up, but remains at or below the striking price throughout the life of the contract, the time premium will decline slowly to zero as time passes, and finally the contract will expire worthless, because it has no intrinsic value, and the option life will have run out.

However, stocks usually do move, one way or another, during the contract period, and so the time premium will also fluctuate according to the speculative interest in the stock and the option (supply and demand at work) and depending on the distance from the striking price, as well as the time remaining in the contract. As the option increases in value (in the money) the time premium shrinks. As it approaches striking price on its way down, the time premium increases in percent of the option price.

The most profit that can be made in options is by purchasing calls or puts and disregarding all the other complicated uses and hedging techniques. An in-the-money option can increase by the amount the common stock moves, with only a fraction of the invested capital it would take to buy the underlying stock. The most that can be lost in an option is 100 percent of the price paid if the option expires worthless. This is one feature of stock options that make them much safer speculative vehicles to trade than commodity futures (where you can be locked in by repeated margin calls when the market has limit moves opposite to your position).

A comparison of how a particular call option might move in relation to a six percent move in the underlying stock with 100 shares of the same stock purchased on margin is as follows:

A $50 stock costs $5,000 per 100 shares and may currently be bought for 50 percent margin, or $2,500 with the rest borrowed from a stock broker at interest. A three month $50 call might be purchased for $3 per share, or $300 plus commission. If the stock goes up to $53 in two weeks, the $50 call might go to 4½ or generate a 50 percent gross profit

($150) on the option, while the value of the 100 shares of stock goes up by $300 (or 6 percent). From this $300 you must pay two commissions and the interest expense on $2,500 for the two week period. You can see that the leverage is greatly increased by the purchase of the call option. If you want to trade, why own the stock when you can lease it for a short-term move? Options are the perfect vehicle for this, and you can operate on a much smaller amount of capital and satisfy your speculative objectives for trading based on your prediction of the underlying stock movement. Note also that 10 percent moves in stock prices often create 100 percent moves in option prices that are near the striking price when positions are opened.

Again, referring to the example above, if the stock were to decline to $49 in the next two-week period, the option might drop to 2¼ and you could still close your position with about two-thirds of your capital intact. It would cost much more to pay round-trip commissions on 100 shares of stock for the same privilege.

A COMPARISON: TRADING THE STOCK VERSUS TRADING THE OPTION

To illustrate how option trading can be far more profitable than trading a stock outright (even when the stock is bought on margin), study Table 1, comparing possibilities for a stock that increases 6 percent and 10 percent in price over a short period of time. Note how the percent profit on investment is so much greater, even for one option contract, and how it increases for five contracts. I have chosen a period of fifteen market days for the example which means that the transaction was opened and closed during that period. You can see the profit potential on an annual basis, if you can time your purchases and sales this well and continually trade puts and calls throughout the year.

PUTS

A "put" option is a contract that entitles the buyer to *sell* shares of a stock (usually 100 shares) at a specific striking price at any time the option is in force. The put option buyer expects the market and the underlying

TABLE 1 Comparison—A Stock Versus Option Trade

	Straight Purchase 100 Shares XYZ	Margin Purchase 100 Shares XYZ (50 Percent Margin)	Call Option Purchase 1 Contract at $3	Call Option Purchase 5 Contracts at $3
Cash Invested	$5,000	$2,500	$300	$1,500
6 Percent Move				
Sell at $53, receive	$5,300	$5,300	$450 (4½)	$2,250 (4½)
Profit *before* deducting commissions, margin interest	300	300	150	750
Less commission and margin interest	172	182	41	149
Net profit	$128	$118	$109	$601
Percent profit on investment, 15 days	2.56%	4.72%	36%	40%
10 Percent Move				
Sell at $55, receive	$5,500	$5,500	$650 (6½)	$3,250 (6½)
Profit *before* deducting commissions, margin interest	500	500	350	1,750
Less commission and margin interest	172	182	45	161
Net profit	$328	$318	$305	$1,589
Percent profit on investment, 15 days	6.56%	12.72%	101%	106%

stock to *drop* in price for his profit. In other words, as the stock drops in price the put holder has the right to *sell* the stock at the striking price. A put option then is the opposite to a call option, since a call option increases in price as the stock advances in price.

Premium values for put options behave similarly to call options. The intrinsic value of a put is the amount the put is in the money, or the amount the stock price is *below* the striking price at which the put was bought. For example, in the previous table if a $50 put was purchased when the stock was at $47 the intrinsic value of the put would be $3. There would also be a time premium added to the price of the put and this amount would be similar to that of a call option that was $3 in the money; but remember that time premium can vary greatly, depending on the speculative interest in the stock at any particular time. If the biased interest is bullish on the stock, the time premiums on the puts are usually less than call time premiums.

Assume that we bought a $50 put for $4½ when the stock price was $47. Note that $1½ would be the time premium in this case. If the stock dropped in price to $44 we might be able to sell the put for $7 for a 55% gross profit. You would expect the time premium to shrink in this case, as the stock moved from $47 to $44, because time premiums decrease as options move deeper in the money away from the striking price.

If, on the other hand, the price of the stock increases to $50 or above at the expiration date of the contract, then the put would expire worthless. Again just as with call options, the put options buyer can only lose 100% of the price paid for the option. You can compare buying a put with shorting a stock and see that there is not only much more leverage in trading the option, but the maximum risk is known.

In order to have a put contract option to buy, there must be a put writer. The put writer receives the premium paid by the buyer, just as in the case of the call writer. The mechanics and techniques for put writing are more complicated than those employed in writing calls. In some cases a put writer may be short the underlying stock and sells a put to partially protect his position in case the stock rises in price. He may also be trying to increase his income on the short stock position, and will keep all of the premium if the put expires worthless.

The put writer is at risk, however, at all times that the stock price is less then the striking price. Remember, the put buyer has the right to *sell* the stock at the striking price. Going back to our example, the put option holder could exercise the option by "putting" it to the writer, and the writer must buy the stock at the striking price regardless of the market price of the stock.

Put positions are closed in the same manner as call positions. If you have bought a put, you can close the position at any time during the contract period by simply selling it. If you are the put writer, the position may be closed by the purchase of a put with the same striking price and expiration date.

OPPORTUNITIES AND SAFEGUARDS FOR OPTION TRADERS

Much becomes clear by studying different series of options, such as the fact that near-term options have greater liquidity in volume of trading, and usually relatively higher premiums, especially those barely in the money or near the striking price. This is because of speculative interest in short-term price changes near expiration. Near-term options are the most active and easiest to trade, since there is a narrow spread between the bid and asked price, but you also have little time to correct a trading error.

Stock option trading would not be possible unless there were active option markets such as the Chicago Board Options Exchange, American, Midwest, Pacific, and Philadelphia Stock Exchanges because it takes active bidding markets to create liquidity for traders. It would be much more difficult to match these orders in the over-the-counter market. Option trading on the exchanges makes smooth continuous trading possible.

All rules and regulations governing the buying, selling, and writing of options are set forth in the *Prospectus of the Options Clearing Corporation*. This prospectus must be carefully read and thoroughly understood by anyone who wants to trade options. In addition, brokerage firms have rules and regulations of their own, and you may have to meet certain of their requirements before you are permitted to trade. All these safeguards are for your benefit and protection, and to screen out those who have no knowledge of the risk of the option market. Those who cannot afford the risk are discouraged from trading in this market.

There are many different option strategies and trading techniques used that are not discussed in this book. Some of these methods (hedging, spreads, etc.) are designed to minimize trading losses while trying to make limited gains based on various assumptions of the future movement of the underlying stock. If you want to learn some of these methods to see how they are used, I suggest the following references for study:

Ansbacher, *The New Option Market*
Davis and Jacobson, *Stock Option Strategies*
Gastineau, *The Stock Options Manual*

FIVE

Mathematics of Continuous Option Trading

For an option trader to make substantial gains (regardless of tax considerations), his capital must be working at all times. When his money is not actually in options, it should be drawing daily interest in a money market fund that has in and out privileges. Most big brokerage firms now have this kind of an account, and you should take advantage of one, so that even when your capital is idle it is drawing interest—compounded daily.

We are all familiar with the concept of compounding. It is only through compounding and rapid turnover of capital that we can truly rack up the big gains. That is why I believe so strongly that if a person does his homework, uses a good mechanical trading system, and develops the discipline necessary to follow rigidly a set of very specific trading rules, he can achieve really fantastic results as an option trader.

An example of compounding capital by trading options that I like to use (and to keep in mind as a sort of personal goal) is the following: if you invested $1000 in ten straight option trades, making a net profit of 30 percent on each trade, your initial capital would grow to $13,786, if all capital were reinvested each successive time. Of course, some trades would yield much more, some much less. (I might add it is extremely unlikely that anyone could accomplish this consistently.) This is the opportunity that drives the serious option trader to study constantly to improve his methods and techniques.

MARKET-TIMING SIGNALS AID IN COMPOUNDING OPTION TRADING GAINS

In Chapter 9 we will introduce the Moving Balance Indicator, a superb market timing device that gives about 8 to 10 buy and sell signals a year for the overall market. I will go into this in much more detail in Chapter 9, but for the purpose of demonstrating the possibilities of compounding using this indicator, I will touch on it briefly now.

Reversal points of the Moving Balance Indicator over the past three years show that there are about 8 or 10 key buy and sell signals within a 12 month period for the overall market. By comparing the MBI reversals with individual stock charts, you can see that most stocks will move approximately in phase with these reversal points and trend changes. If you are trading stocks that have puts as well as calls available, you have at least 16 ideal trading opportunities during the year. As I point out in following chapters, you must wait for these timing signals to occur to make sure you are in phase with the short-term trend and the overall market strength or weakness that moves the Dow Jones Industrial Average by at least five percent.

The MBI signals, and the signals that occur in the charts of individual stocks, can be the basis for the compounding of capital by reinvesting successively in a series of option transactions.

The amount of starting capital in an option trading program is the *least important* factor; the *most important* factor is being able to make a continuing series of transactions while yielding a net profit. This can only be done with a system that gives valid market-timing signals for correct buy and sell decisions.

It is important to remember that some diversification in the options selected help spread your risk. For example, if two options are to be bought it may be better to buy one option on each stock, rather than two options on one of the stocks, all other factors appearing equal.

In order to succeed and have a net gain, you must be right on your buying and selling decisions more than 50 percent of the time. Profit must accumulate and then be taken promptly when a sell signal is given. Losses must be taken quickly to preserve your trading capital.

The following tables, I believe, give reasonable objectives and expectations for 10 completed successive trades, starting with an initial amount of $1000. Assumptions are that all remaining capital is reinvested in the next trade, and that it makes no difference where the losses occur in the series, as long as they are limited to 33 percent. This means, for example, that if a call option is purchased at $3 and declines to $2, it should be sold. You will often want to cut losses shorter than this by following the five-day position rule (you will read about this later), or when any other unpredicted activity causes the stock and option to drop.

SERIES OF OPTION TRADES

With the tables constructed, several things become apparent. The breakeven point if you are right 50 percent of the time, or 5 out of 10

TABLE 2

Number Times Right	Percent Gain in Trade	Number Times Wrong	Percent Loss in Trade	Remaining Capital at End of Series
5	50	5	33	$ 994
6	50	4	33	2,232
7	50	3	33	5,040

TABLE 3

Number Times Right	Percent Gain in Trade	Number Times Wrong	Percent Loss in Trade	Remaining Capital at End of Series
5	60	5	33	$ 1,373
6	60	4	33	3,288
7	60	3	33	7,918

TABLE 4

Number Times Right	Percent Gain in Trade	Number Times Wrong	Percent Loss in Trade	Remaining Capital at End of Series
5	75	5	33	$ 2,150
6	75	4	33	5,629
7	75	3	33	14,828

TABLE 5

Number Times Right	Percent Gain in Trade	Number Times Wrong	Percent Loss in Trade	Remaining Capital at End of Series
5	100	5	33	$ 4,192
6	100	4	33	12,544
7	100	3	33	37,760

times, with a profit each time of 50 percent and five losses of 33 percent, shows that you must do at least that well to stay in the game. Notice, however, from Table 2, should you increase your trading ability to be correct 6 out of 10 times, your capital would increase to $2232, or more than a 100 percent gain in an 8 to 12 month period. Also, during the series you should expect some trades to make more than 50 percent, and that your net profit would climb considerably over this amount if you continued to cut your losses at 33 percent each time they occurred.

The Table 3 projection shows how real profit can start to accumulate when you are right 6 out of 10 times, and your average profit per transaction is at least 60 percent. Note that a good profit occurs when there are four losing trades at a 33 percent loss in the series. These results would then triple your capital in about one year if you were correct seven times, which is a reasonable projection.

Tables 4 and 5 show much greater potential, but, of course, these results are much harder to achieve. Look at what happens when 75 percent profits are made and you are right 6 or 7 times out of 10! Obviously to operate in Table 4 or 5 your stock and option selection, as well as market timing, must be really superb. Therein lies the potential in option trading. I do not know if anyone has ever accomplished results like these, but who can say whether these goals and results are impossible?

I cannot emphasize enough that the key to obtaining results in the option market is for you to check all points before making a buy or sell decision. Losses must be taken promptly to preserve your trading capital and to get you into a position for the next trade where your decision will have a better chance of being correct. If your losses are allowed to run 50 percent or more, your trading capital will soon be exhausted, taking you out of the market. This has happened to me many times because I have not obeyed the rules and stayed with losing positions.

Stopping losses quickly is a major key to winning in the option game. If you do your homework on all the other aspects of trading that I present in this book, and if you take small, quick losses, you will be successful in accumulating profit over the long term. One of the best mental attitudes you can develop is a willingness to take a loss and free your mind for the next opportunity. If you are able to predict six or seven correct moves out of 10 initial positions, getting an incorrect trade out of the way *increases your chances of being correct the next time.* This is the attitude and approach I finally developed, and now I always get a better feeling after selling out a losing position.

PART TWO

How You Can Acquire the Technical Skills That Form the Basis for the Stewart System of Short-Term Option Trading

If you are a person who does not have a computer, who does not have minute-to-minute access to market quotes, who cannot spend all your time following your trades, then you need to have some way you can keep up with your trading on a day-to-day basis. Your best tool, and one that all of us have access to every day, is the daily newspaper. If you read *The Wall Street Journal* every morning, you have all the data you need to begin acquiring the skills I use. By setting aside a little time each morning to find out exactly where you are in terms of the market, the stocks that you follow, the trades you are involved with, and the general psychological climate of the marketplace, you will be able to start the day feeling more comfortable in your option positions. You will not be constantly distracted during the day worrying about them.

In Part Two I take you through the learning process *I* went through, and share with you the best of the technical tools and ideas that I have been able to find—the ones that became the basis of the Stewart System. I explain them briefly, then list the sources of this material and tell you where you can read further about these subjects. Later, in Part Three of the book, I explain how these ideas fit together into an overall plan for short-term option trading.

My trading techniques have evolved over the years from an early interest in stock charts, through the study of every book on technical analysis I could get my hands on, to experimenting with my own stock charts to which I added some of the best of the technical ideas I had gleaned from my studies.

Chapter 6 introduces the reader to stock charting, and offers him an idea of the usefulness of stock charts as well as how they are commonly interpreted.

As I gained some experience and became more knowledgeable through trial and error (losing some money along the way), I realized that simply charting my stocks told me where I had been but gave me few clues to future action. Critics of charting frequently make this point, and it is valid—one cannot rely solely on past chart action for decisions about the future. You must also have some predictive tools.

The need for a way to predict probable future action led me to explore the *cycles* of both individual stocks and the market as a whole. There is identifiable, constantly repeating cyclic motion—hills and valleys—of differing time spans (days, weeks, months, years) at work in stocks and in the market. By projecting the approximate time span of past cycles into the near future, one can make a pretty good guess as to where these cycles are most likely to top or bottom out in future time. A concept related to cycles is that of *trading envelopes.* Definite boundaries (called envelopes) can be drawn enclosing all of the trading action. What appears at first to be a random movement of stock price now becomes a clear picture of the trading range with the cycle reversal points meeting the envelope boundaries. Thinking in terms of cycles and trading envelopes will add greatly to your ability to guess what the future trading action is likely to be. This material is dealt with in Chapter 7.

A discussion of *moving averages* and how they can help us to identify the underlying trend of a stock is presented in Chapter 8. Moving averages can give buy and sell signals. They can confirm when a trend is over or has reversed. You can construct moving averages yourself to reveal whatever underlying data you wish to see on your charts.

Many market analysts and writers of stock market advice use the terms *overbought* and *oversold,* but most laymen do not have a clear idea of what they mean. Chapter 9 will explain these terms and show you how important it is to be aware of these conditions. When the market (or a stock) is becoming dangerously overbought, a drop in prices will occur soon. When extremely oversold conditions exist, a rise in the market (or a stock) is predicted. In this chapter you will learn to construct your own market oscillator, called the MBI, so that you will always have some idea of where you stand in relation to the overall condition of the market, what part of the short-term cycle you are dealing with, and when a top or bottom has formed—signaling a change of direction. When you know you are in phase with the market, you will have peace of mind, a sense of relief, and a feeling of self-confidence.

Measuring the volume of trading (that is, the number of shares that change hands each day in a stock or the market) is discussed in Chapter 10, as well as two systems for measuring *supply and demand,* or *accumulation/distribution,* on your stocks as you record daily price action. I present *my* version, the Stewart Accumulation/Distribution Index, which you can learn to plot for yourself using the stock quotes out of the newspaper. How I interpret it gives you more valuable clues as to what is really going on in a stock, and what may be about to happen.

Analysis of the Dow Jones Industrial Average is another useful way to keep your finger on the pulse of the market. Since the DJIA represents a large part of the total dollar value of all shares traded on the New York Stock Exchange, it is useful to keep track of Dow cycles and the accumulation/distribution patterns in the Dow as a further indicator for improving your market timing. Your individual stock does not have to be a Dow stock. Most stocks move with the market and the Dow to some extent (except when an unusual news story is breaking—falling earnings, a merger in the works, and so forth—or when a very strong move is underway that defies what the rest of the market is doing). It pays to keep an eye on the Dow, and compare its cycles with those of the stocks you are tracking. Chapter 11 shows you how to plot accumulation/distribution on the Dow and by combining it with the MBI market oscillator, provides a very powerful and effective market timing tool.

Chapter 12 presents the most effective way to select the stocks you want to follow on a day-to-day basis for option trading signals.

With the skills, indicators, and methods presented in Chapters 6 through 12, you should have a very comprehensive basis for applying technical analysis to short-term option trading. This is the cream of the crop—the best I have been able to assemble over the years. I have discarded an awful lot of very expensive books that were worthless to me. You have probably done the same. When I attend an occasional market seminar now, hoping to hear something new from some currently popular market guru, I usually find I know more than he presents about market timing and stock selection for option trading—and, for me at least, my methods are far more reliable and easier to use.

I don't want to give the impression that I think technical analysis is foolproof, or that a strictly technical approach is the whole story. An awareness of psychological factors, current events, good judgment, and nerves of steel (!) are needed. Changing fundamental factors must be taken into consideration as well. You don't want to ignore such factors as impending earnings announcements, expected dividend dates (which affect stock prices), stock splits, and so forth.

After you have acquired some familiarity with the concepts presented in Chapters 6 through 12, I will show you how to use them as a basis for the Stewart System, and show you how to put it all together—in Part Three.

SIX

Stock Charts – A Visual Picture of Past Trading Action

The old adage that a picture is worth a thousand words is certainly true when one is trying to get an idea of a stock's history and its probable future movement. A number of excellent books have been written about the analysis and use of stock charts and their value in predicting stock movements. They are referred to by fundamentalists as well as technicians, but it is the technician who relies most heavily on the charts (and other technical data) for his forecasts on future price trends.

There is a school of thought that the market is a *random walk* (i.e., totally random in movement with no underlying relationship to chart phenomena) and cannot be forecast by any method. All that can be said for those who follow this approach is that their accounts will balance out to zero if they attempt to trade the option market in a random fashion in support of their theory. Of course, these "mathematicians" would not be in the options market in the first place, since they consider the odds no better than those provided by the laws of chance. It is my intention to show you that this is not true.

The option trader must know how to read and interpret charts if he is to be successful in the market. In no other way can he get a feel for support and resistance areas, trend-channel changes, major tops and bottoms, breakouts from consolidation patterns, and many other clues to future stock action.

Obviously, a book on option trading cannot provide a complete course in chart analysis. Therefore, in this chapter and throughout the book, I give you examples of how chart interpretation can help you and possibly whet your interest for further study.

Two excellent books in the field of stock charting are the classics by Edwards and Magee entitled, *Technical Analysis of Stock Trends,* and William Jiler's, *How Charts Can Help You in the Stock Market.* These texts came out in their original editions many years ago, but they are both still valid today. A recent new book, *Investors Guide to Technical Analysis,* by C. Coburn Hardy, also has some brief, well-written comments on charts taken from other authors describing chart patterns and other technical information. If you do not already have a good knowledge of the subject, I recommend that you study a few good texts on chart analysis. The books listed above are not difficult to understand and will give you more self-confidence and insight in making trading decisions. You can probably find one or more of these books on the shelves of your local public library or bookstore.

The imaginary chart for the XYZ Corporation, Figure 1, shows some of the most common chart patterns relied on by technical analysts. Those shown are especially helpful to the short-term option trader. It should be pointed out that the patterns presented here are in very simple form to give the person unfamiliar with charting some idea of how charts can be useful. In actuality, many of the patterns will be more complex and require a much longer period of time to develop.

As daily trading in XYZ is recorded on our hypothetical chart, it has been sluggish for some time up to now. It has had very little price movement and very low volume—not a very interesting stock—then, one day:

1. From the *support zone* of 20, a breakout occurs on the upside (a buy signal is given). The stock moves into an *uptrending channel,* which remains intact until the *trendline* is broken, at which time a reversal in trend occurs (a sell signal is given).

2. After trending downward briefly, a *rectangular consolidation pattern* forms, right at the old support level of 20, suggesting that perhaps the selling pressure is off and a rise in price may be forthcoming. This is also taken as confirmation of support at 20. Sure enough, a breakout from the consolidation occurs (a buy signal). A sharp rally follows, on higher volume, but runs

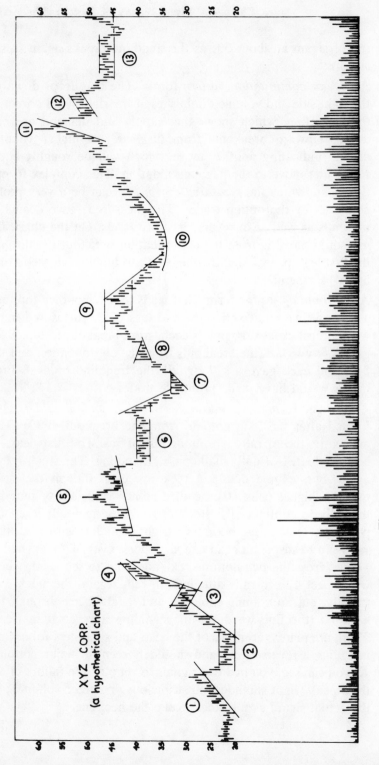

Figure 1. An imaginary chart for the XYZ Corporation.

out of steam at about 33, as the trendline breaks again (a sell signal).

3. A *flag,* or *continuation pattern* forms. The flag drops down on the right side and volume diminishes at the right-hand corner of the formation, which shows that supply and demand are balanced. Upward breakouts from flags are on higher volume, usually indicating another move, which will be roughly equal to the first move to the flag consolidation. This complex formation is known as the *measured move,* and can be a very profitable one for the option trader. The measured move occurs in uptrends as well as in reverse in downtrends. On the chart, the measured move is from the consolidation breakout (2) through the first leg up, included the flag (3), and finally, the second leg up to 44, where:

4. An *uptrending wedge* forms that leads to a temporary top, and a reversal in trend. Notice the two legs of the measured move were almost exactly 10 points each, from breakout to top. Each gave a *buy signal* (the breakouts from the consolidation and the flag) and each gave a *sell signal*(the trendline breaks). Both moves would have made profitable trades.

5. A reversal formation, known as a *head and shoulders,* has formed after the long uptrend from the breakout at (2). This means the recent rally is running out of gas. The first peak, or left shoulder, is usually made on high volume. The stock rallies again, but volume does not pick up, even though the stock makes a higher peak (the head). Lacking sufficient volume for the rally to continue, the stock drops back again. It is at this point, where a second bottom (or right shoulder) is formed, that we begin to suspect a head and shoulders reversal. We pencil in a line across the two bottoms, extended out to the right, where we suspect a third rally attempt will fail. Again, the stock tries to rally, but no volume comes in and it falls back through the *neckline* (the line we drew in), signaling a reversal in trend. There are many variations of the head and shoulders formation, including a reverse head and shoulders seen at major bottoms. As you can see, you had two signals to get out: the failure of the third peak (right shoulder) on suspicious or lighter volume, and the actual signal as the stock broke the neckline.

6. This is another rectangular consolidation with a breakout on the upside, but this one is a treacherous example known as a *bull trap,* because what looked like the start of a promising rally broke down and fell through the consolidation, breaking out on the downside instead. Only close monitoring of stock action can keep you from being sandbagged by a bull trap. If you had been watching carefully, the drop off in volume and the pullback through the consolidation area would have suggested getting out as the stock broke the bottom line of the rectangle.

7. After this downtrend appears to slow, an *ascending triangle* forms. (The top line is horizontal, the lower line rising to meet the horizontal at a point to the right.) Ascending triangles usually indicate the stock is being accumulated again, fewer and fewer shares are being offered for sale and these are at higher and higher prices and rising bids. Someone is buying up to, but no higher than, the level of the horizontal line. Finally, demand overcomes supply and the stock breaks out on the upside, giving a buy signal. This can be a very reliable signal to watch for, especially after a substantial sell-off.

8. This is a continuation pattern called a *symmetrical triangle,* shown here breaking out on the upside. The stock usually continues to move in the direction of the breakout. This can be seen in the middle of a measured move, as in the earlier example, and indeed, this whole rally could be considered another measured move.

9. The *double top formation,* or *"M" formation,* is a top reversal pattern that is very common. The first peak is made on high volume. The stock pulls back, another rally begins, but volume does not develop. Selling comes in and kills off this rally attempt, too. A downtrend is signaled when price drops below the center point of the "M." This formation is also seen in reverse at bottoms, forming a "W," the actual signal being to buy when you see the price breakout above the center peak of the "W."

10. Here we have a consolidation referred to as a *saucer bottom.* These formations usually form after a considerable time has elapsed in which there is very little interest in the stock and there is no more selling. Gradually, a little bit of buying appears

—just enough to curve the line upward very slightly. Little by little, people begin to accumulate the stock again, and the line curves up more sharply. Soon we have a full-fledged rally and smooth curving trend upward culminating in:

11.   A *climax top,* characterized by an *exhaustion gap, high volume,* a *one-day reversal,* followed by a sharp slide. The stock has hit a *resistance area* (the price at which no one else wants to buy) and is exhausted by the last gasp of upside volume. The very next day, the price falls right through the gap that occurred on the way up, and continues to fall as people sell, and sell short, and as stop-loss orders are triggered. A one-day reversal says, "get out quick."

12.   This looks like a continuation of the previous rally, but note that there is no increase in volume; the stock forms an upward slanting flag (continuation pattern), this time pointing higher. This is only a *technical rebound,* a short-lived rally in a continuing downtrend. These almost always fail, and break out on the downside. This is our old friend, the *measured move* again, this time in a downtrend. Note the two approximately equal legs in this sell-off.

13.   A rectangular consolidation, with a breakout to the downside. This quickly reverses, however, forming a *bear trap,* and goes up through the consolidation area again, the reverse of the *bull trap* seen earlier in (6). Some traders would obviously sell short on the downside breakout, only to have to cover at higher prices as the stock reversed to the upside, thus *trapping* the bears. Again, close watching by the astute chartist would limit losses and not fool him for very long.

There are many other chart formations that can be studied. When you have studied some of the books on chart analysis you will have a much better feel for recognizing the chart patterns as they occur. It is also important to study the volume characteristics of the formations to increase your understanding and to develop a sense of the supply and demand in a stock. You will begin to notice when changes in volume subtly start to alter the course of a stock's movement. In general, a stock in an uptrend should move up on higher volume and consolidate on lower volume. Just the opposite occurs in a down move. Technical rebounds usually are on smaller volume and are of short duration, especially in severe bear market moves.

Study and interpretation of stock charts are very valuable visual tools for short-term option trading, but charts alone are not the complete answer for proper timing. They should be used with other technical and timing techniques discussed in this text to get as complete a technical picture as possible on the status of a stock. These timing tools include cycle analysis, trading envelope boundaries, accumulation/distribution, the Moving Balance Indicator, and so forth. Obviously, you must also have current up-to-date information on which to base your decisions, as out-of-date data is of no help in predicting short-term movements.

Of course, everyone has good 20-20 hindsight when reading charts. The art and technique comes when you are trying to predict the immediate future from past action, and this is a difficult task. It is a good feeling, however, to get the timing and analysis to the point that you are right about 7 or 8 out of 10 times (and sometimes you can capture even greater moves than you had predicted with your work). This is part of the enjoyment of successful short-term trading. (Of course, spending some of the money you have made is part of the enjoyment, too!)

SEVEN

Cyclic Motion of Stocks

Many people believe that stocks move in a random fashion, thus making it impossible to predict the future by the past. The study of stock charts and of the market itself, however, will show that cyclic patterns do occur and, in many cases, with amazing regularity over a period of time. Of course random events, such as a fundamental change in a company, unexpected earnings reports, or a merger offer, do create unpredictable moves. This, however, does not eliminate the cyclic movement for the average stock or for the overall stock market itself. A study of several stock charts showing a history of at least one year will visually show you cyclic patterns at work.

The best reference I have studied on cycles in the stock market is the book written in 1970 by J. M. Hurst, *The Profit Magic of Stock Transaction Timing*. This detailed and definitive study of cyclic phenomena on stock movement should be read to gain a thorough knowledge of the subject.

Briefly, Hurst's work shows that there are no less than 12 cyclical components at work in a stock, or the Dow Jones Industrial Average, or other indices, at all times. These cycles are present and can be identified as far back as we have market data from which to construct charts. For our purposes we shall comment on the cycles of most interest to us as potential option traders.

For the last 30 years, a cycle of 4 to 4½ years duration (on the average) has been evident in the market (see Figure 2). This cycle is variously referred to as the "bull-bear" market cycle, the business cycle, or the

47

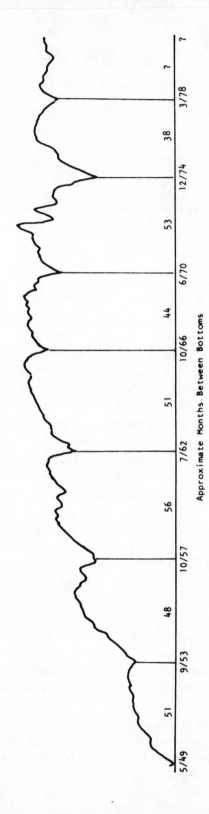

Approximate Months. Between Bottoms

DOW JONES INDUSTRIAL AVERAGES --- THE 4 - 4-1/2 YEAR BULL/BEAR OR BUSINESS CYCLE

For the last 30 years, a cycle of 4 - 4-1/2 years duration (on the average) has been evident in the market. This cycle is variously referred to as the bull/bear cycle, the business cycle, or the economic cycle. It is tied closely to the expansions and contractions in our economy, the presidential election term, and other factors. It is the cycle most referred to and analyzed by stock market experts.

Figure 2.

48

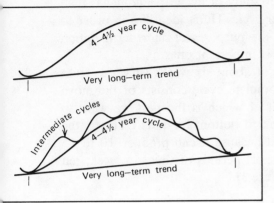
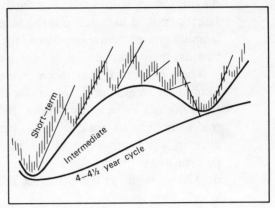

Figure 3. (*a*) Very long-term trend, business cycle and intermediate term cycles added. (*b*) Short-term cycles added to the intermediate-term and business cycle.

economic cycle. It is closely tied to the expansions and contractions in our economy, as well as to the presidential election term. For our purposes, we will refer to it as the *long-term cycle* (keeping in mind that there are other, longer-term cycles at work that we will not be dealing with here). The cycle, December 1974 through March 1978 (only 38 months compared with the average length of about 51 months) may represent what Hurst calls deviation in relative magnitude and duration. Variation in length of cycle is likely to be the result of the summation of other, longer-term cycles at work (see section on Summation of Cycles). So far this current business cycle has not behaved characteristically, either—so perhaps a different dominant cycle is beginning to emerge. One other interesting detail you might note—the period from May 1949 through December 1974 appears to be one big 24½ year cycle.

The second cycle we will consider in future chapters is the *intermediate-term cycle,* with a duration of many months, superimposed on the long-term cycle (see Figure 3).

SUMMATION OF CYCLES

Figure 3 demonstrates how the sum of several cycles of different duration tend to exaggerate movements at times, and flatten them out at other times. Only three of the many possible cycles are shown, so the diagram is oversimplified. For further study of cyclic phenomena, read Hurst's book. I have left out the other cycles Hurst identifies in order to simplify my presentation, since, for the purposes of short-term option trading, these three cycles are the most important ones.

There is a third, *short-term, cycle* of about six weeks (it varies from four to six weeks) in duration. (A complete cycle consists of the move from bottom to peak to bottom, half of which is the part we want to trade—bottom to peak for calls, peak to bottom for puts.) This is the cycle in which we are most interested because it can produce 10 to 15 percent moves in the stock price in short periods of time—a week, ten days, three weeks at the most (see Figure 3).

USE A CHART SERVICE FOR CYCLE ANALYSIS

The use of a weekly chart service provides a quick and easy way to select and analyze stocks for option trading. By learning a few simple techniques you can determine the cycles you wish to trade, how long a short-term move is likely to last, and where your buy and sell points are likely to occur.

The best cycle to work with for option trading is the short, four to six week cycle. To identify this cycle enclose the action of the intermediate cycle within a constant-width envelope. From the chart of IBM, Figure 4, you can see that the 10 to 15 percent moves usually occur within 10 to 20 trading days from the reversal points of the intermediate trend. This is the cyclic motion in the stock that Hurst says contains about one-fourth of all stock motion. When we add this fourth to the already established intermediate and long-term uptrends sometimes already in effect, the amount of potential gain in one short-term move can be truly astonishing! (See the December 1978 move in Figure 4.) This is what Hurst calls "the summation principle." The effect is at work in down-trends, too (see the June 1979 move in Figure 4).

The approximately 10 to 15 percent short-term moves in a stock correspond to the movement of the market in general. The internal strength or weakness of the market tends to move both market and individual stocks from peak to valley and back again in a regular cycle. (This corresponds to the conditions *overbought* and *oversold,* which we will take up later in Chapter 9.)

Another reason for this short-term cyclic motion might be that active stock traders who buy at the start of a move (or reversal point) tend to take profits when a 10 percent move has been completed.

In studying the past price history of a stock, it is easy to enclose the stock price action within a constant-width envelope including almost all of the trading price range (see Figure 5).

This is a technique that can be developed quickly with a little practice. You do not have to be too detailed in order to get a good approximation of the envelope width of any particular stock. The prior history, when enclosed in the upper and lower envelope bands, gives you the predicted price limits likely to continue in the immediate future. Many times the lower edge-band tends to control the boundaries of the stock trading range. At other times this is done by the upper band, as the stock tends to trade closer to this edge. You should mentally picture that the stock will trade in the zone between the two bands you have constructed.

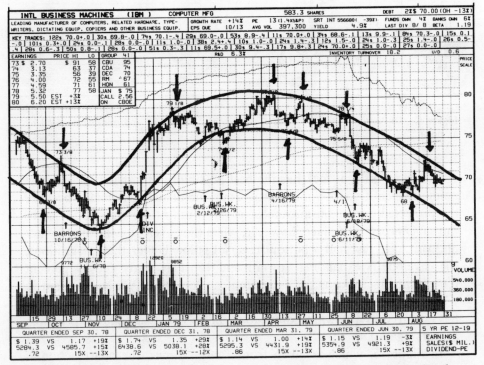

Figure 4. IBM chart showing envelope and cycle points. Courtesy of *Daily Graphs*, P.O. Box 24933, Los Angeles, Calif.

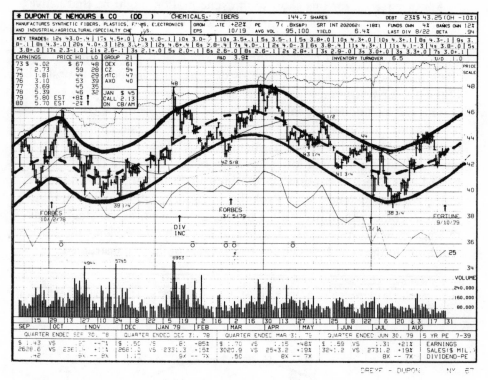

Figure 5. DuPont chart. Courtesy of *Daily Graphs.* (Envelope and mid-band added by author.)

In other words, a stock has the best possibility of moving the greatest amount when it starts a movement from one of the edge-bands because the projected maximum movement is the width of the envelope. Larger movements can take place, however, when the envelope is turning higher and you have just had a bottom reversal point. Under these conditions, the envelope is expanding upward and you can easily get 20 percent movements in stocks as the ascending envelope gives you more room in which to move up. The reverse can be true after a top edge-band reversal has occurred in a downtrending stock. (This is the summation principle at work again.)

In Figure 5, which is taken from *Daily Graphs,* the chart action is first outlined as presented to determine the intermediate envelope. Note that the boundaries of the constant-width envelope are about 10 percent of the stock price. When the stock price hits the edge-band, or boundary, a reversal trend usually starts, moving the stock price toward the opposite boundary to fill the price envelope.

By extending the boundaries of the envelope forward in time on your chart, you can see what the limits of probable future action will be. If the long-term trend has been up, assume it will continue up and draw your lines slanting upward. If the stock appears to have made a major top or bottom, extend your lines to accommodate a change of direction. If the envelope has been trending downward, your lines should slant downward. It is always safest to assume that the recent trend will continue, unless you have strong reasons to suspect a change is coming. Do not try to forecast too far into the future—for our purposes (short-term option trading) the next few weeks is sufficient. Or, when a cyclic component of a certain duration, three weeks, six weeks, and so forth, has been noticeable in the recent past, it is safe to project at least that far ahead to anticipate the approximate point of the next cycle top or bottom.

The charts should be updated weekly to revise estimates to accommodate the past week's action, to project new ones, and to take into account the overall strength or weakness of the market. Be sure you also take into account the effect of possible changes in direction of the intermediate and long-term cycles. This is where using major trendlines and moving averages can be helpful (see Chapter 8).

After this is done, you will want to mark past reversal points and estimate points for near-term future reversals of the stock within the intermediate envelope (see Figure 4). The points that hit the edge-bands are the buy or sell points for options. These are not exactly periodic, but it is amazing how regularly they do occur over a time period. These times and prices then become action points when supported by other data, such as the Moving Balance Indicator and the Accumulation/Distribution Index which are explained in other chapters.

Finally, draw in the *trend-channel* for the anticipated move (see Figure 6). As soon as you have a few days' data, connect the bottoms of the daily price action (either on your own daily charts, or in your chart service book). This establishes the trendline. (Connect tops in downtrends.) Draw a line parallel to the trendline which will approximately connect the tops and enclose all the price action inside a *channel*. (For down moves, the parallel line is drawn below the trendline.) You may

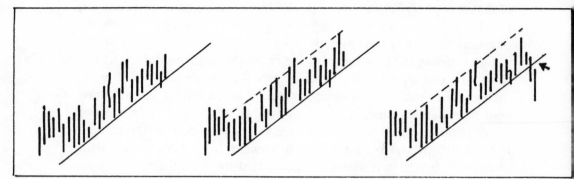

Figure 6. Trendlines, trend-channels, and trendline breaks.

have to adjust these lines slightly as the move develops. If the trendline *breaks,* and the other measurements we will consider later are negative, you must get out of your option positions immediately. This will be discussed further in later chapters.

Cycles must be considered as major forces working on stocks to produce price changes. They *must not* be ignored if you want to improve your timing. If they are ignored, you will be out of phase and will usually incur a loss immediately. Most people are inclined to buy when rallies are underway rather than buying after declines. The opposite discipline must be developed to take action at the right, rather than the wrong, time.

WATCH DOW CYCLES, TOO

In addition to looking at the individual stock in which I want to trade, I also enclose the Dow Jonees Industrial Average each week with a similar envelope. Note from Figure 7 how the Dow Jones Industrial Average itself moves in about a 40 point, or 5 percent, range as determined by the vertical distance between the lower and upper band. There are short-term cyclic reversals from upper and lower boundaries, and there are also *major* reversal points that indicate a change in the intermediate and long-term trends. It is important, therefore, when you update your charts each week, that you also update the Dow, paying *particular* attention to any suspected change in the intermediate trend.

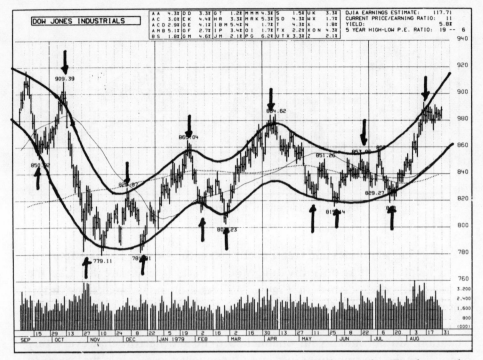

A A	4.3%	D D	3.3%	G T	1.2%	M M M	4.3%	S	1.5%	U K	3.3%
A C	3.0%	E K	4.4%	H R	3.3%	M R K	5.3%	S D	4.3%	U X	1.7%
A C D	2.9%	G E	4.1%	I B M	5.4%	N	1.7%	T	4.3%	X	1.8%
A M B	5.1%	G F	2.7%	I P	3.4%	O I	1.7%	T X	2.2%	X O N	4.3%
B S	1.8%	G M	4.6%	J M	2.1%	P G	6.2%	U T X	3.3%	Z	2.1%

DJIA EARNINGS ESTIMATE:	117.71
CURRENT PRICE/EARNING RATIO:	11
YIELD:	5.8%
5 YEAR HIGH-LOW P.E. RATIO:	19 -- 6

Figure 7. Dow Jones Industrial Average. Courtesy of *Daily Graphs.* (Envelope and arrows added by author.)

This envelope on the Dow then gives you a picture of the overall stock market itself and will add to your confidence as to where the market average most likely will be next week or perhaps for the next three weeks. There are exceptions, but on balance *you cannot trade against the overall action and trend of the Dow Jones Industrials or Standard & Poor's 500,* and be successful—you *must be in phase with these overall market movements.*

Observe how many leading stocks move approximately in phase with the Dow Jones Industrials. This is to be expected because these large industrial issues make up such a great part of the dollar value of all shares traded on the NYSE each day. At times, secondary issues can have runs that greatly exceed the movement in the Dow, but the high-priced, high-quality stocks have plenty of price movement themselves to make good option trades.

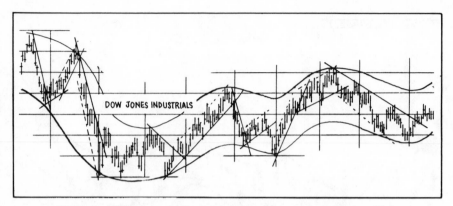

DOW JONES INDUSTRIALS

Figure 8. Dow Jones Industrials with envelope and trendlines added.

Marking trendlines and trend-channels on the Dow is just as important and helpful as it is on individual stock charts (see Figure 8). Use the same method described in Figure 7. Trend-channel breaks are interpreted the same way for the Dow or for any other index. A break in the trendline usually is a signal to get out—a reversal is forming. A word of caution: do not make your channel so tight and narrow that every tiny move breaks the trendline; just loosely connect those points that seem to be in a line, and ignore any tiny tips that do not fit.

SUMMARY: WHY YOU MUST CONSIDER CYCLES

Enclosing stocks in constant-width envelopes helps us to see the long-term and intermediate-term cycles clearly. It is important to get a mental picture of a stock's past action to enable you to project into the future, and here a picture (or chart) is certainly worth a thousand words. You must build a framework for expected moves, and you must be thinking about the near-term future, that is, the next *5 to 15 trading days,* before an option position is taken. This cannot be done without studying the immediate past price action and the trading parameters of the stock. (The 5 to 15 days referred to represent an estimate of half of the next short-term cycle—from cycle reversal point, or buy signal, to the halfway point, or top, of the expected short-term cycle. Needless to say, some cycles may be longer or shorter.)

The established envelope gives you the expected limits of the short-term moves and helps you to see the short-term cycles at work, independent of the long-term cycles. The principle of summation helps you anticipate whether the move will be strong or weak. You should update your charts weekly, and project the cycles forward in time to anticipate the approximate future reversal points. You should establish trendlines and trend-channels, and be alert for trendline breaks.

Cyclic analysis of the Dow helps to confirm that your stock is in phase with the market, and whether the market is strong enough to support a broad rally.

Catching a movement that starts from the edge-band of the stock's envelope provides the greatest potential for a short-term option trade.

Do not worry about the occasional random move that can occur and upset the normal cyclic prediction. Large gains or losses can be made from these unexpected moves and they must be considered part of the opportunity or risk that is inherent in any short-term option or stock position. This also suggests the wisdom of some diversification in the selection of option positions to better balance this risk. Putting all your capital in one position is not wise and can be disastrous if the unexpected happens.

EIGHT

Moving Averages— Another Timing Tool

DEFINITIONS AND CONSTRUCTION OF MOVING AVERAGES

Moving averages, as applied to stock charts and market data, are lines that are plotted in conjunction with actual prices. An average is calculated for a given number of data points and plotted on the stock chart (or other charted data). The average "moves" as a new value is added and an old one subtracted each day, giving a new average point to plot.

The two most commonly used moving averages found on published stock charts (see Figure 9), are the 50 day moving average and the 200 day moving average.

A moving average is a "smoother." Its purpose is to act as a filter, straining out the confusing detail often seen in a sequence of numbers so that the underlying *trend* is revealed. For stock chart analysis, the 50 day and 200 day moving averages suit the needs of most traders and investors because they provide trend information considered important in the selection of stocks.

A 50 day moving average (ten weeks of five market days each) eliminates, or filters out, *short-term* fluctuations in price, allowing us to see the *underlying intermediate-term trend*. It also calls our attention to the trend that underlies the much shorter cycles we are interested in for short-term option trading.

The 200 day moving average (40 weeks of 5 market days each) eliminates all the short-term and most of the intermediate-term action, thus exposing the long-term trend. If both of these moving averages are turn-

59

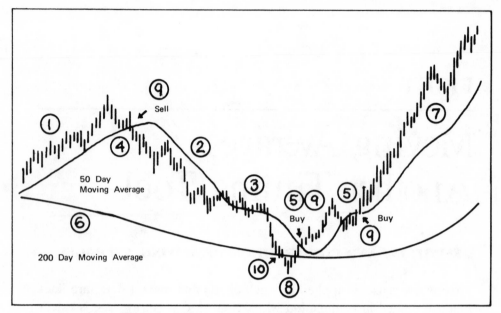

Figure 9. Moving averages reveal underlying trends.

ing up, or already rising, we can feel more confident that our stock is in an uptrend for the intermediate and longer term. The reverse is true for a downtrending moving average or a moving average that has turned down.

The chartist infers a number of things from a moving average (see Figure 9). Some of the more common interpretations are:

1. The price action of a stock in an uptrend will ride above the moving average line.

2. The price action of a stock in a downtrend will ride below the moving average line.

3. A stock that is neutral or undecided in direction will cross back and forth many times over its moving average line. The line itself will tend to go sideways.

4. When a stock's price action crosses through an uptrending moving average line, it may indicate the stock is reversing direction and is headed down.

5. When a stock's price action crosses through a downtrending moving average line it may indicate the stock is reversing direction and is headed up.

6. The longer the time span of the moving average, the smoother the line. While a 200 day moving average will give you the long-term trend, a 50 day moving average will show you the intermediate-term trend.

7. When a stock's price action rises very far above its moving average line, a return to the line or reversal in price will come soon. (A stock seldom stays for very long at a great distance above its moving average line.)

8. The reverse is true when a stock's price falls a great deal below its moving average line. A move up to meet the line can be expected.

9. Buy and sell signals are given when price-action crosses the moving average line.

10. A crossing of the long (200 day) time span may indicate a major change of trend.

Moving averages can be applied to other numbers in time sequence to smooth out irregular data, and to identify changes in trend. For instance, if you are keeping a chart of daily market statistics (stock prices, commodity prices, or sequential data points of any kind), you may find when they are plotted in graph form that it is difficult to identify any underlying trend (see Figure 10).

By selecting the right moving average, the short-term peaks and valleys can be smoothed out to let the trend show through and, at the same time, give us timing signals.

If we want very short-term signals for the overall market, as we do for option trading and to calculate the MBI (see Chapter 9), we use the 10 day moving averages which eliminate the daily fluctuations of less than ten days, but give us a smooth line to plot in conjunction with the original data.

To construct a moving average we must first gather the selected number of data points. (For a 10 day moving average, 10 numbers; for 50 day, 50 data points; 30 week, 30 weekly statistics, etc.) The appropriate number of data points are tabulated, totaled, and divided by the number

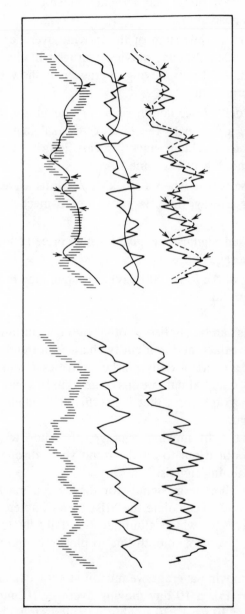

Figure 10. Choose the average that allows the information desired to show through.

TABLE 6   10 Day Moving Average, Closing Stock Prices

Date	Closing Price	10 Day Total	10 Day Moving Average
7/02/79	58.25		
7/03	58.75		
7/04	holiday		
7/05	57.25		
7/06	58.875		
. . .			
7/09	58.0		
7/10	59.25		
7/11	58.75		
7/12	59.25		
7/13	58.75		
. . .			
7/16	59.5 =	586.6 ÷ 10 =	58.7
7/17	60.0	588.375	58.8
7/18	60.25	589.875	59.0
7/19	59.5	592.125	59.2
7/20	59.75	593.	59.3
. . .			
7/23	60.5	595.5	59.6
7/24	61.0	597.25	59.7
7/25	61.5	600.0	60.0
7/26	60.875	601.625	60.2
7/27	61.75	604.625	60.5

of data points used, resulting in our first average number to be plotted (round off to one decimal point). This number is plotted on the day of the last data point. Thereafter, each day (or week for weekly data) the new daily figure is *added* to the 10 day total, and the oldest daily figure *subtracted* in the series. Dividing by 10 and rounding off gives the next point, or "moving average" to be plotted (see Figure 11).

A simple table showing how to construct a 10 day moving average based on the daily closing price of a stock appears below. The 10 day was selected for simplicity, but the same methods are used no matter what span of time is selected.

By penciling in plus and minus signs by the numbers as you add and

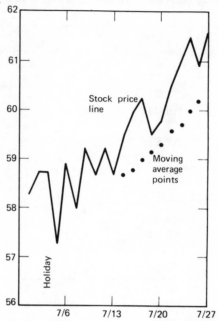

Figure 11.   10 day moving average, closing stock prices.

subtract them, you can easily keep your place in the tabulation from day to day, and avoid making errors. You can be sure that you have used the correct number when you have marked it in this manner, and feel confident that you have not skipped one or used one twice. In the event you feel you do have an error, or may be subtracting the wrong number, the easiest way to check it is this: take your 10 day total at whatever point you want to start (on our table, say, July 18, 589.875), add to this total the next day's closing price (July 19, 59.5), count back eleven days from the new figure (July 19) which gives you the number to be subtracted (July 5, 57.25). Now you are back in business with a correct audit and you can continue the series, being sure to mark plus and minus each time. A different colored pencil can be used the second time; this will differentiate between the first set of marks and the second and will also remind you that you have checked the numbers, and even tell you exactly where you started your check.

Moving averages can be devised to smooth out any data, or to allow you to examine information not readily apparent in the raw figures and to provide signals for action. For more sensitive signals for short-term use, you must devise a moving average with a shorter time span.

It is possible you may want a five day moving average in some cases, as I have used on the MBI (see Figure 19, Chapter 11). In this case I take the MBI values, which are all based on 10 day moving average data, then calculate a five day moving average of this average to give better and shorter-term trend changes which are extremely important in identifying MBI reversals.

In *The Profit Magic of Stock Transaction Timing*, J. M. Hurst applies moving averages of varying time spans to identify recurring cycles in a stock. His work is detailed and explains moving averages in mathematical terms for anyone who wants to know how they work, why they work, and how to devise and interpret them. Again, I recommend this excellent book to anyone interested in understanding chart phenomena, cycles, and many other aspects of technical analysis.

The previous paragraphs describe moving averages as they are conventionally used. Understanding their use gives you a better understanding of the underlying trends that have been in effect and are either still in effect or are changing direction.

USING MOVING AVERAGES IN TRADING OPTIONS

Now that we have discussed what moving averages are, how they are constructed and interpreted, how can we use them to analyze stocks for option trading?

First, and most obviously, by using them in the conventional way they give changes in trend, buy and sell signals, and alert us when the stock is extremely overbought or oversold (when price has moved far away from the moving average line).

Historically, the 50 day moving average changes direction two or three times per year when plotted for the Dow Jones Industrials or the Standard & Poor's 500. The rounding tops and bottoms formed by these moving averages will be present in most stocks, also. You can have greater confidence in predicting the course of the intermediate-term trend in the future if you will make a habit of studying the moving averages on the Dow and the Standard & Poor's 500 as well as that of an individual stock.

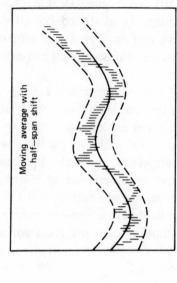

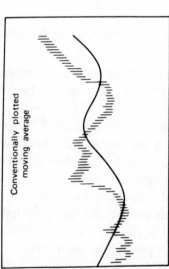

Figure 12. How the 50 day moving average can be used as an envelope mid-band.

THE HALF-SPAN SHIFT

Hurst, in his previously mentioned book, explains that the *true* time relationship between the moving average and the data it smooths is *not* the one used by published chart services. The last data point is not associated with the current price, says Hurst, but with a point *one-half the span of the moving average—in the past*. For more effective interpretation, the moving average should be shifted one-half of its time span back in time (to the left). For a 50 day moving average, this would be about 25 days. The shift allows the major reversal points in the moving average to line up with the stock price reversal points where they actually occurred (see Figure 12) and causes the moving average line to *bisect exactly* the constant-width envelope on the trading action!

Of course, you will have no moving average points plotted for the most recent 25 days, and the moving average as plotted this way will run *right through* the price action instead of riding above or below as it does when conventionally plotted. Remember, if you *do* use this moving average with the half-span shift back in time, some of the conventional rules stated in the first part of this chapter will not apply.

THE HALF-SPAN USED AS A MID-BAND

I have developed a technique based on the half-span shift which is very useful in establishing reversal points and boundaries of constant-width envelopes, and in estimating the near-term future price action. When I look at the 50 day moving average line on a published stock chart, I *mentally* shift it 25 days to the left, which will line up major reversal points in the moving average with corresponding reversal areas in the stock price. I then try to establish a *mid-band* for the constant-width envelope which approximates this moving average line with a one-half span shift. The outer boundaries of the constant-width envelope can then be accurately drawn in, connecting cycle tops and bottoms, and the envelope extended into the probable future trading zone.

Figure 13 shows the price range for Digital Equipment between August 1978 and August 1979. The heavy 50 day moving average line in

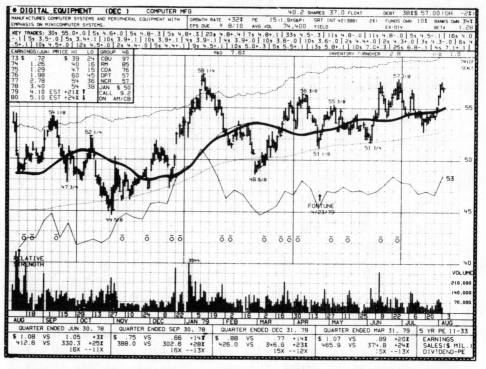

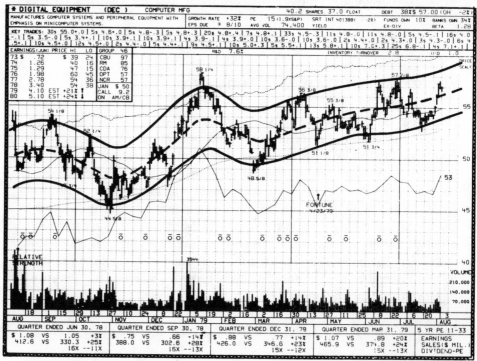

Figure 13. (*Top*) 50 day moving average line (emphasized by author). (*Bottom*) Envelope and mid-band (added by author). Charts courtesy of *Daily Graphs*.

Figure 13a indicates that the stock had three major reversal points during that time. This means the moving average reversed direction three times during the year, reflecting changes in the direction of the intermediate-term trend. Figure 13b shows the same chart with a mid-band (represented by a broken line) and envelope boundaries sketched in. Notice how closely this mid-band line approximates the 50 day moving average line *if* that line were shifted one-half span or twenty-five days to the left!

If you make a practice of establishing a mid-band within the trading envelope and compare it with the published 50 day moving average line (with a mental shift of 25 days to the left), you can be more confident that your envelope boundaries are correct, and you can more accurately project them into the near-term future—the time span in which you plan to trade options. If the envelopes are kept up to date on a weekly basis with the mid-band added, you can develop a continuing line that will show trend reversal points nearly as well as actually calculating the moving average yourself and then plotting it with a half-span shift.

Estimating the mid-band on a weekly basis is very helpful in determining the slope of the intermediate trend and in verifying just where within the envelope boundaries near-term trading is likely to take place.

If you are plotting the moving average yourself, you will find that when the data is shifted 25 days to the left and plotted, you can actually get a better picture of major turning points in the intermediate trend than if you plot the new average point at today's date.

The half-span delay works with any moving average. By simply dividing the length of the average in half, and plotting it in that time relationship—for example, a 15 day moving average should be plotted with an 8 day lag in time, and so forth—a mid-band can be established for any data.

Personally, I find the mental shift serves my purposes just as well as actually plotting the moving average and saves a lot of time.

PULLBACKS AND TECHNICAL REBOUNDS

Two of the rules mentioned in the early part of this chapter (items 7 and 8) deserve special emphasis. When a stock moves sharply away from its moving average line, especially due to a news announcement, panic selling, or speculative interest, it will return at least part of the way toward its moving average line. These are the extremes of price action that we described as overbought and oversold in Chapter 9. If an envelope is drawn to include this price action, you will find it turning sharply up (or down) with the price breaking through the established edge-bands. If the move has been on the upside and the stock has gone way above the moving average line, a sharp correction (or pullback) of approximately one-third to one-half of the recent move can be expected. Then the stock may resume its uptrend. When a situation like this develops on the downside, with the stock dropping sharply below its 50 day moving average, you can expect a sharp correction (or technical rebound) to occur which will recover approximately one-third to one-half of the recent move.

Sometimes excellent trading profits can be made by watching this phenomenon when stocks plunge twenty percent or more in a matter of two days on a news announcement and become extremely short-term oversold. Your timing must be exactly right for capturing the ensuing *technical rebound* and these positions are normally closed out within one to three days after purchasing. The main thing to look for is interday trading action where the stock churns in a narrow price range as the news is fully digested in the market. The price should then stabilize on heavy volume before positions are taken and you can expect an immediate rebound of one-third to one-half towards the previous trading range before the downtrend may resume.

The *pullback* from extremely overbought conditions can also be traded in stocks that have *put* options. Again, this works in reverse from the technical rebound in a sharply falling stock. In this case, the stock *rises* very sharply on a news story or wild speculation, pauses to digest the news, profit-taking sets in, causing the stock to drop sharply back toward its moving average line, usually by one-third to one-half of the recent rise in price. This may be a very short-lived move, and the strong uptrend may resume immediately. These put option positions must be taken very quickly, watched carefully, and closed out promptly—sometimes in only a day or two—very risky positions, not to be undertaken by the fainthearted!

TRADING TECHNICAL REBOUNDS
IN DOWNTRENDING ENVELOPES

From my own experience I have found that trading technical rebounds in sharp downtrending envelopes when the 50 day moving average is biased down is extremely difficult with long calls. The technical rebounds that do occur from the oversold conditions are rather sharp, but they are not extensive and normally there is not more than a five to six percent move in the stock before it approaches its 50 day moving average line, and then rapidly turns down and continues in the downtrend. As stated earlier, it is possible to trade these technical rebounds within the downtrending envelopes, but you have little margin for error.

Also, as explained in the other parts of the text, the Moving Balance Indicator, the lower edge-band of the envelope, and the accumulation/distribution of the stock must all be in phase before a long position is taken in a downtrending envelope. These are the only opportunities you have to trade calls in a primary bear market trend for most stocks, and you must realize that when you do you are trading against the tide. A much better strategy is to trade with the intermediate trend by purchasing *puts* at the correct time instead. Many more puts have been made available for trading recently, so now we have a much larger selection of stocks from which to make safe profits in a downtrending market.

TAKING CALL POSITIONS IN GENERAL

In general, you usually do better trading call options when the 50 day moving average has definitely made a rounding bottom turn and is headed up. It will give you a greater degree of confidence if both the envelope and the moving average of the stock price is moving up at the same time. This reinforces your projection that the stock will move higher and will be in phase with its intermediate cycle, when the overall market is ready to move.

You should observe both the 50 day and the 200 day moving average lines in the weekly edition of a chart service, such as *Daily Graphs,* to improve your mental picture of probable trading direction for the near-term future.

The published 50 day moving average line is helpful in trading, not only for the intermediate trend, but also to better define the gradual forming of top and bottom trading zones by using it as a mid-band in establishing the constant-width envelope. Learn to use and refer to this line as another important technical indicator in your arsenal.

NINE

Measuring Overbought/Oversold Conditions in the Market

One statement about the stock market that no one will argue with is the market will fluctuate. In addition to this, for the short term the market and stock will tend to move within a trading range, or envelope, as it progresses in a longer term uptrend, a neutral or sideways pattern, or a longer term downtrend.

In the short term, the market and a given stock will oscillate about a central trendline within the channel or envelope that bounds the price action. The upper and lower limits of the boundary contain the usual expected cyclic action and correspond to the technical conditions called overbought or oversold (see Figure 14).

The market forces react to bring the buying and selling back toward a central point between the two extremes, and this restores a balance point to the price and movement of the stock. The short-term fluctuation is the distance from the upper boundary to the lower boundary of the price envelope. The midpoint is a continuous line of balanced stock action.

Larry Williams, author of *The Secret of Selecting Stocks for Immediate and Substantial Gains,* defines an *overbought* stock as one in which approximately two-thirds of the traders are eager buyers and one-third are sellers. An *oversold* condition technically occurs when there are two-thirds sellers at the market and about one-third buyers. This represents

73

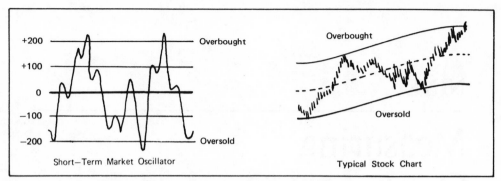

Figure 14.   Measuring overbought/oversold in the market or a stock.

buying or selling pressure within an issue. Obviously, there are never 100 percent buyers or 100 percent sellers at any one time or price. If this were the case, there would be no transaction. Williams defines the percent buyers, or buying pressure, as the distance between the low and closing price of the stock during a particular day's trading. Percent selling is defined as the distance from the high to the close of that day with, of course, volume as part of the magnitude of buying or selling. (This is discussed in more detail in Chapter 10).

SHORT-TERM OSCILLATORS MEASURE OVERBOUGHT/OVERSOLD

Several chart services print a short-term market oscillator, but again, as with published stock charts, you can be four or five days out of date each week while you wait for the next chart book. If you received your chart book on Monday morning, it is up to date through the previous Friday. But, what if the mail is slow? (This happens all the time—sometimes my chart book arrives on Wednesday, or not at all—you know how the U.S. mail is!). Current, day-to-day information is necessary for the close timing needed for short-term option trading.

DR. LLOYD'S MOVING BALANCE INDICATOR

During my years of studying and trying to understand market fluctuations, I have tried all kinds of indicators and oscillators. Finally I found

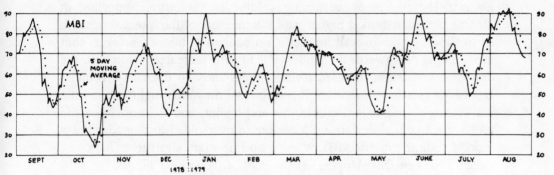

Figure 15. The Moving Balance Indicator for 1978–1979.

one that is extremely reliable, useful for short-term trading, and, best of all, one that I could calculate myself on a daily basis. It is the Moving Balance Indicator (MBI), presented by Dr. Humphrey Lloyd in his book *The Moving Balance System—A New Technique for Stock and Option Trading.*

If you keep this short-term market oscillator yourself, on a *day-to-day* basis, you will always know precisely how the overall market stands in regard to being overbought or oversold, and you will see the turning points coming. Lloyd's MBI is a very important tool, and I want to go into it in detail so you can see how it works, why it works, and how it relates to the other components of my method. You will also be able to construct it for your own use. The MBI for 1978–1979 is shown in Figure 15.

The MBI combines three basic ways to measure what is happening in the day-to-day changes in the market as it oscillates between the extremes of overbought and oversold.

The first element, the *Advance/Decline Index,* is based on the number of advancing stocks versus the number of declining stocks traded each day on the NYSE. [This is not to be confused with the NYSE Advance/Decline Line (see Glossary) which appears on some market charts, and with which most of us are familiar.] More about this element later.

The second element is volume. Volume is the engine that moves stocks and the market in general. You can observe any long-term stock chart and see that strong upward moves are nearly always accompanied by big expansions in the trading volume. Obviously it takes increased interest and buying demand to clear overhead supply and move stocks upward. Volume tends to decrease on declines in an upward or neutral trading market. The degree of advancing volume is, therefore, important in moving the stock market higher, and is a measure of the internal strength or weakness of the overall market. Consequently, in stock markets that are trending downward, the tendency is toward increased volume on the downside with short, upward technical rebounds on decreased volume. It is easy to see how important it is to know how much fuel (volume) the market engine has as it climbs higher and higher, and to know when the fuel is giving out, forewarning a decline to oversold. Lloyd incorporates market volume into his MBI by using an important short-term indicator called *The Ten-Day Moving Average of Advancing Volume.*

The third element of the MBI is the *Trader's Index.* This index is constructed by dividing the number of advancing issues by the number of declining issues. The advancing volume is divided by the declining volume. A ratio is then calculated by dividing the first result by the second. The Trader's Index is

$$\frac{\text{advances}}{\text{declines}} \div \frac{\text{advancing volume}}{\text{declining volume}}$$

At any one time this answers the question, are the advancing issues getting their share of the volume of trading? A ratio of 1.00 indicates a neutral and balanced market. A ratio of less than 1.00 indicates a stronger market and extremes in this ratio are about 0.4 for a very strong market and about 2.0 for a very weak, or bearish, market. Therefore, small numbers are bullish and larger numbers are bearish in this index.

Lloyd's MBI (Moving Balance Indicator) combines the short-term trading data in the overall New York Stock Exchange as follows:

1. Ratio of the 10 day moving average of the advances divided by the 10 day moving average of the declines, which he calls the A/D Index.
2. 10 Day Moving Average of Advancing Volume.
3. 10 Day Moving Average of the Trader's Index.

The Moving Balance Indicator, derived from the three indices above, has ranged between 25 and 105 during the 1977, 1978, and 1979 time periods according to my calculations. The information for calculating the MBI is taken daily from *The Wall Street Journal* where it appears on the inside of the last page, upper right-hand side, in a box under the heading, *Market Diary* and the last paragraph in the same box, *Trading Activity*. When plotted, it contains all of the factors necessary to give an accurate picture of the internal strength or weakness of the market on a short-term basis.

The following tables show 30 days of calculations for the MBI.

Table 7, the A/D Index, is a ratio of the 10 day moving average of advances divided by the 10 day moving average of declines, times 10. In calculating all 10 day moving averages, first record the data for 10 days. Total the 10 days, and divide by 10 to get the 10 day average. On the eleventh day, add the eleventh day value to the *10 day total* and subtract the value recorded 11 days ago from it. Then divide by 10 and this gives you the 10 day average for the most *recent* 10 day period. Each day the new value is added to the 10 day total, the one 11 days ago is subtracted. The *new* 10 day total is divided by 10 producing the new 10 day average. As these values are calculated daily, they become the 10 day moving average. Be sure to mentally multiply the daily result of the A/D Index by 10 (shift decimal point one place to the right) and record on Table 11.

Note: The MKDT symbol on the Bunker Ramo equipment gives the advances and declines, the MKDV symbol gives the advancing and declining volume, and the MKDS symbol gives the short-term trading or Trader's Index, if you want to obtain the daily information from quotation machines at the close of the market. Be aware, however, that this will not give you the composite final totals you will find in the next day's *Wall Street Journal*. The figures will be close enough for our purposes, but to be consistent I would suggest using one source or the other on a regular basis.

Table 8 is the 10 Day Moving Average of Advancing Volume. It uses the NYSE total number of shares advancing, which you will find under *Trading Activity* in the *Wall Street Journal* box mentioned earlier. Record the advancing volume daily, rounding off the last three digits (for 17,650,000 shares, record 17,650), and construct a 10 day moving average, as you did in Table 7. Divide the resulting daily average figure, for example, 15,447, by 1000—just move the decimal point three places to the left—and record the result, 15.447, on Table 11.

Table 9 is the 10 Day Moving Average of the Trader's Index (MKDS). See previous page for how to figure the *Trader's Index*. Lloyd has given *assigned values* to the 10 Day M.A. MKDS to produce a plotting value that would combine with the results of the other two elements to make one composite index, the MBI. Since the first two indices were direct indicators (up equals up), and the MKDS is a reciprocal indicator (up equals down), he used this method to turn the MKDS into a direct indicator like the other two, and at the same time gave it a value that, when combined with the other two, produced an index (MBI) that closely represented percent buying power or percent selling power, as it moves between the extremes of overbought and oversold. His assigned value of 8.5 (MKDS = 0.75) would indicate a strong market, and a value of MKDS = 1.80 gives an assigned value of minus 2.0, or a very weak market. The assigned value of 6.0 (1.00 MKDS) represents a neutral market. When a daily assigned value MKDS figure has been calculated, it is entered on Table 11, with the results of Tables 7 and 8. (See Table 10 to convert MKDS to the assigned value.)

Table 11 is the calculation of the MBI itself. The A/D Index, the 10 Day Moving Average Advancing Volume, and the 10 Day Moving Average MKDS are added together and multiplied by two. Lloyd's reasons for multiplying by two are: (1) to round off the numbers to the nearest whole number more easily and accurately, and (2) to bring the figures into line with the percent buying and selling pressure. A high (80) MBI would suggest 80 percent buyers, 20 percent sellers; a low (20) MBI would suggest 80 percent sellers and 20 percent buyers—for the time period in 1974 and 1975 when he was calculating the values for his text.

In addition to the above original MBI tables, I like to use a fifth, Table 12 which is a 5 day moving average of the MBI itself, which helps to confirm that the tide is changing from overbought to oversold, or the reverse. On the chart of the Dow with the MBI (see Figure 19, Chapter 11), the 5 day moving average on the MBI is represented by the dotted line.

Note that when the MBI turns from down to up, or up to down, the moving average points tend to cluster as a trend change is developing. In like manner, most of the tops are also called by the bunching of 5 day moving average points that are then penetrated by the MBI itself as it turns down. This moving average gives buy and sell signals that are quite accurate most of the time.

I have plotted the MBI for over three years and have found it to be very reliable in helping predict the short-term direction of the overall market. There are times when you will get an interruption in the MBI before its final top or bottom that can cause you to take wrong action, but these signals rarely occur.

You will also see from studying the chart of the MBI (see Figure 15) that the peaks tend to be about 6½ weeks apart, whether in the high or low range. There are exceptions to this, with some reversals occurring in as short as four weeks and some running as long as 10 weeks between reversal points. At any rate, you should expect a reversal within those time zones, but do not take action until the trend changes direction.

When the MBI is used properly *with other technical timing tools,* and action is taken as indicated, you will not be trapped in losing positions and your timing will be greatly improved for entry points in buying call or put options. Normally the MBI takes three to four days to make a reversal, although they are sometimes very sharp in nature. In my opinion, this is the best overall short-term indicator to measure the strength, weakness, and direction in the market at any particular time.

This may seem too complicated to keep up with on a daily basis, but I assure you, once you have mastered it, the necessary calculations take only a few minutes each morning and are well worth the effort, considering the peace of mind it allows you.

TABLE 7 A/D Index

Date	(1) Advances	(2) Declines	(3) 10 Day Moving Average Advances	(4) 10 Day Moving Average Declines	(5) A/D Index	(6) × 10
7/2	431	1102				
3	826	590				
5	802	539				
6	1086	390				
9	1004	496				
10	666	820				
11	577	884				
12	481	967				
13	524	900				
16	824	594	722	782	0.992	9.92
17	424	1066	721	725	0.996	9.96
18	469	976	686	763	0.898	8.98
19	790	614	684	771	0.888	8.88
20	777	605	654	792	0.825	8.25
23	572	834	610	826	0.739	7.39
24	820	594	626	803	0.779	7.79
25	1088	407	677	756	0.896	8.96
26	802	598	709	719	0.986	9.86
27	778	556	734	684	1.073	10.73
30	776	663	730	691	1.055	10.55
31	998	480	787	633	1.244	12.44

To calculate, run a 10 day moving average of advances (column 1) and put the results in column 3. Run a 10 day moving average of declines (column 2) and put the results in column 4. Divide the 10 Day Moving Average Advances (column 3) by the 10 Day Moving Average Declines (column 4), and put the results, the A/D Index, in column 5. Multiply the A/D Index times 10, and enter figure in column 6, and on Table 11.

TABLE 8   10 Day Moving Average of Advancing Volume NYSE

Date	Advancing Volume	10 Day Moving Average Advancing Volume	Divide By 1000
7/2	5,740		
3	16,750		
5	17,360		
6	27,320		
9	27,630		
10	13,550		
11	12,930		
12	7,070		
13	10,360		
16	15,760	15,447	15.447
17	5,570	15,430	15.430
18	12,950	15,050	15.050
19	11,640	14,478	14.478
20	13,530	13,099	13.099
23	10,400	11,376	11.376
24	14,230	11,444	11.444
25	24,990	12,650	12.650
26	16,060	13,549	13.549
27	13,030	13,816	13.816
30	14,910	13,731	13.731
31	21,170	15,291	15.291

To calculate, run a 10 day moving average of the daily NYSE advancing volume, divide result by 1000, and enter result on Table 11.

TABLE 9   10 Day Moving Average MKDS

Date	MKDS	10 Day Moving Average MKDS	Assigned Value
7/2	1.525		
3	0.801		
5	0.740		
6	0.643		
9	0.734		
10	1.167		
11	0.961		
12	1.413		
13	0.971		
16	0.607	0.956	6.4
17	1.696	0.973	6.3
18	0.669	0.960	6.4
19	1.176	1.004	6.0
20	0.810	1.020	5.8
23	0.819	1.029	5.7
24	0.842	0.996	6.0
25	0.592	0.960	6.4
26	0.878	0.906	7.0
27	0.959	0.905	7.0
30	0.767	0.921	6.8
31	0.836	0.835	7.7

TABLE 10   10 Day M.A. MKDS —Assigned Value

10 Day Moving Average MKDS	Assigned Value	10 Day Moving Average MKDS	Assigned Value
0.76	8.4	1.32	2.8
0.78	8.2	1.34	2.6
0.80	8.0	1.36	2.4
		1.38	2.2
0.82	7.8	1.40	2.0
0.84	7.6		
0.86	7.4	1.42	1.8
0.88	7.2	1.44	1.6
0.90	7.0	1.46	1.4
		1.48	1.2
0.92	6.8	1.50	1.0
0.94	6.6		
0.96	6.4	1.52	0.8
0.98	6.2	1.54	0.6
1.00	6.0	1.56	0.4
		1.58	0.2
1.02	5.8	1.60	0.0
1.04	5.6		
1.06	5.4	1.62	−0.2
1.08	5.2	1.64	−0.4
1.10	5.0	1.66	−0.6
		1.68	−0.8
1.12	4.8	1.70	−1.0
1.14	4.6		
1.16	4.4	1.72	−1.2
1.18	4.2	1.74	−1.4
1.20	4.0	1.76	−1.6
		1.78	−1.8
1.22	3.8	1.80	−2.0
1.24	3.6		
1.26	3.4	1.82	−2.2
1.28	3.2	1.84	−2.4
1.30	3.0	1.86	−2.6

Value = −10 (10DMA) + 16

83

TABLE 11   Moving Balance Indicator Table

Date	A/D	10 Day Advancing Volume	10 Day MKDS	Total	Total × 2 = (MBI)
7/10					
11					
12					
13 ~~15~~					
16	9.92	15.447	6.4	31.77	63.53
17	9.96	15.430	6.3	31.69	63.38
18	8.98	15.050	6.4	30.43	60.86
19	8.88	14.478	6.0	29.36	58.72
20	8.25	13.099	5.8	27.15	54.30
23	7.39	11.376	5.7	24.47	48.93
24	7.79	11.440	6.0	25.23	50.46
25	8.96	12.650	6.4	28.01	56.02
26	9.86	13.549	7.0	30.41	60.82
27	10.73	13.816	7.0	31.55	63.10
30	10.55	13.731	6.8	31.08	62.16
31	12.44	15.291	7.7	35.43	70.86

TABLE 12   5 Day Moving Average MBI

Date	MBI	5 Day Moving Average MBI
7/10		
11		
12		
13		
16	63.53	
17	63.38	
18	60.86	
19	58.72	
20	54.30	60.39
23	48.93	57.47
24	50.46	54.89
25	56.02	53.18
26	60.82	54.34
27	63.10	56.98
30	62.16	58.74
31	70.86	62.82

TEN

Accumulation/Distribution: Another Index for Measuring Supply and Demand

Many years ago Gerald Loeb, in *The Battle for Investment Survival,* pointed out that the stock market was really a contest in which stocks moved from *weak hands* into *strong hands* and were later distributed back, at higher prices, from the strong to the weak. He described the day-to-day action in the stock market as a battle between these forces, both fundamental and technical.

Let's look further into this. *Strong hands* are on the *smart money* side of the market. They are the informed insiders and professional people who are closest to the true fundamentals of the industry. They include the stock exchange professionals, the floor traders and the specialists. Over the long term they are going to buy low and sell high. *Weak hands* are the average investors, or outsiders, who act on earnings announcements, broker's or other touts, and general market enthusiasm. They are more likely to buy at high prices, become discouraged, and sell at lower prices. This cycle repeats itself throughout market history.

When a stock has had a period of consolidation and there appears to be no more significant selling, the *smart money* begins to accumulate the stock in anticipation of a coming rise in price. The stock is said to be under *accumulation* as long as there are more buyers coming in and the stock is rising. Accumulation continues until a change in sentiment occurs, and the buying dries up—changing the condition of accumulation to one of *consolidation, top-out,* or *distribution*.

Distribution is the condition in a stock (or the market) that develops after buying dries up. The selling pressure becomes greater than buying pressure and prices drop. The stock is said to be under distribution when more selling than buying is occurring. Distribution (selling and selling short) by the smart money begins close to the top, before the general public is aware that the tide has changed. Distribution continues so long as there are more sellers than buyers.

The above describes long-term accumulation/distribution patterns. The same conditions are present in the short-term moves. Imagine a picture taken by a camera from a great distance with a wide-angle lens, and with the foreground out of focus. This is accumulation/distribution at work on the long-term market cycle. If we "zoom" in for a close-up, we will see that the short-term cycles (the foreground in our picture) also display the conditions of accumulation/distribution within the longer-term cycle. This is the accumulation/distribution we want to focus on for short-term option trading.

GRANVILLE'S "ON BALANCE VOLUME"

The most important technical work on detecting accumulation or distribution at work in stocks has been formulated by Joseph E. Granville and explained most recently in his excellent book, *Granville's New Strategy of Daily Stock Market Timing for Maximum Profit*. Granville's index is called the "On Balance Volume" (OBV). It is a cumulative tabulation of total daily volume on a plus or minus basis over a long period of time. The stock trading volume is recorded daily and *added* to the cumulative total if the stock's closing price is *greater* than yesterday's close. The volume is *subtracted* from the cumulative total if the stock closed *below* yesterday's close. This gives a continuous day-to-day series of numbers that is either in a rising, neutral or falling trend and from which one can predict intermediate and longer term swings, identify breakouts, tops and bottoms, and derive other technical information. Although Granville's OBV is presented in statistical form the numbers can easily be charted if you prefer a visual approach.

Granville has shown that over a long period of time, changes in direction of this index, which encompass all of the trading volume in the stock, actually determine whether stock is moving from strong to weak hands, or in other words, whether the stock is being accumulated or distributed by the smart money side of the market. This essentially becomes a supply/demand picture of a stock, either rising for long-term appreciation, or topping and indicating lower prices after a long-term run up. The accumulated net plus or minus volume line is just as important as the price chart in predicting the future stock movement. The "on balance volume" figure is now compiled and used by many investors and fund managers who are interested primarily in the intermediate or long-term trends for fundamental positions. It can also be used for predicting short-term trends, but I feel it is more important for indicating the intermediate and long-term outlook.

WILLIAMS' ACCUMULATION/DISTRIBUTION FORMULA

Another sensitive accumulation/distribution formula was presented by Larry Williams in his important text published in 1972 entitled *The Secret of Selecting Stocks for Immediate and Substantial Gains.*

The Williams' accumulation index is obtained by subtracting the open from the close and then dividing the result by the high minus the low, times the volume for each day's trading in a stock. This formula appears as follows:

$$\frac{(\text{close} - \text{open})}{(\text{high} - \text{low})} \times \text{volume} = +/- \text{ figure}$$

If the open is lower than the close, the net volume figure for the day will be a plus, or buying pressure. A close lower than the opening price gives a minus figure for the day indicating selling pressure. The resulting plus or minus figure is added or subtracted from the cumulative total, and plotted on the chart.

Williams defines the distance between the high and closing price as the selling pressure, and the distance between the low and closing price as the buying pressure for the day. The key to his method is that the plotted line occasionally *diverges* from the price action of the stock itself, revealing what the smart money is doing and predicting either upward or downward movement of the stock trading zone (see Figure 16).

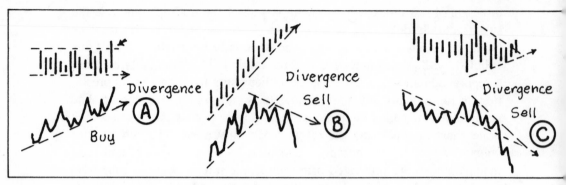

Figure 16. Examples of divergence.

For buy points, a lack of selling pressure (the line refuses to go down any more) is just as important as strong accumulation for predicting a change of trend from down to up. When selling pressure is off you may be reasonably sure a reversal is near. (The reverse is true when buying pressure stops, and the line refuses to go up anymore—distribution has begun and you had better sell quickly!)

This index can give a significantly different picture from the chart action of a stock when they are viewed together. When the accumulation/distribution line moves in a manner contrary to that of the price action line, *divergence* becomes apparent.

Strength in the accumulation/distribution line, which is not reflected in the price action, suggests that the stock is under accumulation. Buy when stock starts to move out of consolidation [Figure 16(A)]. Weakness in the line when none is apparent in the stock action suggests distribution is already occurring [(B) and (C)]—sell.

The difficulty with plotting the Williams Accumulation/Distribution Index, however, is that you must have the opening price of the stock each day in order to compile it, and this becomes time consuming since the opening price is not now published in *The Wall Street Journal,* or other newspapers. If you are charting fifteen stocks on a daily basis a busy broker gets tired of your daily calls for openings. It also presents problems when you are out of town, unable to call, or the quote computer is out.

After studying and experimenting with the Granville OBV and the Williams Accumulation/Distribution Index, I decided neither one met my needs exactly. The OBV did not have the inter–day sensitivity to buying and selling pressure that the Williams Index had, and the Williams Index had the disadvantage of requiring the opening price, which I did not want to bother with.

STEWART ACCUMULATION/DISTRIBUTION INDEX

To combine the best attributes of both indexes, I have developed an index which I call the "Stewart Accumulation/Distribution Index for Short-Term Trading." For short-term trading of stock or options you must determine the technical condition of the stock in relation to its buying or selling pressure. You then must determine whether it is in a temporarily oversold or overbought condition, depending on which position you want to take.

Using the morning newspaper, with yesterday's final consolidated figures, use the following formula: net change from previous day's close, divided by the high minus the low, times the volume equals a plus or minus figure for the day. In other words,

$$\frac{\text{net change}}{\text{high} - \text{low}} \times \text{volume} = +/- \text{figure}$$

This daily figure is plotted cumulatively under each stock that I chart. The figures should be obtained from the daily newspaper using the consolidated trading figures, rather than just those from the New York Stock Exchange. This ratio is easier to calculate than the Williams, since you do not need the opening price each day from your broker as required in the basic Williams formula.

The *net change* in the formula is the difference between yesterday's close and the close of the day before, and is given at the end of the quotation line as a plus or minus fraction ($+\frac{1}{4}$, $-\frac{3}{8}$, etc.). If the net change was a *plus*, the calculated figure will be a *plus*, indicating accumulation. If the net change was a *minus*, the calculated figure will be a *minus*, indicating distribution. The net change fraction is converted to a decimal and is rounded off (i.e., $\frac{1}{4} = 0.25$, $\frac{5}{8} = 0.63$, etc.). The *high* minus the *low*, means the stock's high price during the day minus the stock's low price during the day. The ratio (*net change* divided by *high minus low*) has a limit value of 1.0 as a maximum in my system.

In the event the stock has a *gap* in trading, this ratio can become *greater* than 1.0, but I use 1.0 as a limit for plotting purposes because I am only trying to plot trends and not absolute values with this index. (A *gap* on a stock chart indicates that the stock opened at a higher or lower price than it had traded on the previous day. This will leave a blank space, or gap, in the trading pattern where no traces took place.) *Volume* in the equation refers to daily volume traded in hundreds of shares.

The results of each day's accumulation and distribution are plotted cumulatively on the line, either plus or minus depending on the daily value. Wide swings can develop in this line on a day-to-day or week-to-week trading basis caused by high volume and strong price action days that occasionally occur. A convenient scale to use is one-half inch equals 1000. I prefer to use Keuffel & Esser graph paper No. 47–1322, (10 × 10 to the half-inch), for plotting daily charts. Dietzgen No. 340D, (20 × 20 to the inch) is the same. If you find the accumulation/distribution line running off the paper all the time, you can change the scale, but it is easier to keep all your charts on the same scale so you do not have to think about each one.

Usually the accumulation/distribution line will plot close to the same shape as the Granville OBV, or the Williams Accumulation/Distribution line, although it is obtained by a different method of calculation.

HOW TO INTERPRET STEWART
ACCUMULATION/DISTRIBUTION

The accumulation/distribution line normally takes the same course as the action of the stock, and this can be seen by studying the charts in the final chapters of the book. As mentioned, the high volume, big price change days do alter this index to a large degree, but usually it stays within some bounds, just as the stock trades within an envelope or cycle.

After a period of net accumulation, that is, approximately 10 to 15 days for short term, you can usually expect either a consolidation or a reversal in trend in the accumulation/distribution line, which helps define a short-term top. In many cases, a one or two day top can be predicted by a downward change in the index, especially when it is in the expected time zone for its short-term trend change, because of the cyclic motion of the stock.

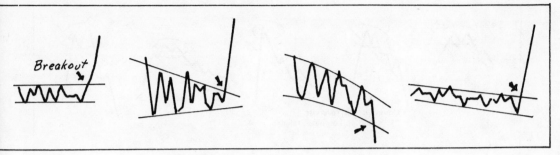

Figure 17. Breakouts from consolidations.

After a period of net distribution in the accumulation/distribution line, a bottom pattern will form. The stock price action will near the bottom envelope boundary. These two things will happen approximately when the trend is likely to change from down to up, as predicted by our cycle analysis. If the MBI is making a bottom also, and is in oversold territory, you have further confirmation that a buy signal is at hand. Wait for the signals before taking a position: trend-channel break on the upside in stock price action, breakout from bottom reversal in the accumulation/distribution line, confirmation of an up move beginning in the MBI.

Heavy volume causes the accumulation/distribution line to break sharply—accumulation makes it go up, distribution makes it go down. Volume moves price, so you need to see a decisive change in this line to assure a good move. Without volume coming into a stock, it is not likely to go very far.

Consolidations frequently form in the accumulation/distribution line when the tide is changing. The consolidations are pictured in Figure 17. Note that there are many possible variations.

Compare the formations in the accumulation/distribution line with possible chart patterns developing in the price action line. A triangle, flag or other pattern in one is sometimes present in the other. When you study the charts in Chapter 16 you will see many examples of this occurring.

Reversals in the accumulation/distribution line usually occur at the same time as in the price action line. Sometimes they occur *ahead* of stock price, giving you advance warning. Reversals will also probably be forming in the MBI at the same time (see Figure 18).

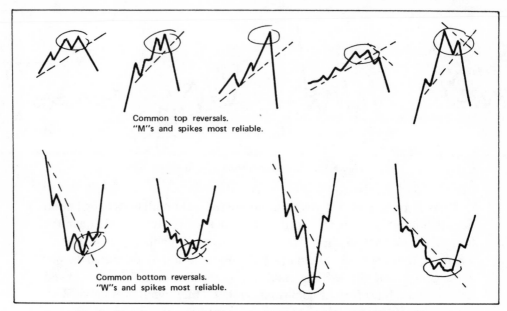

Common top reversals.
"M"'s and spikes most reliable.

Common bottom reversals.
"W"'s and spikes most reliable.

Figure 18. Common reversal patterns in accumulation/distribution line.

A stock sometimes develops a characteristic way of forming reversals. The same pattern will repeat over and over. Watch for these. Some stocks always seem to change direction with a one day reversal which makes a sharp spike, caused by a big burst of volume (down one day, up the next). For examples in Chapter 16 see Hewlett-Packard, Figure 28 and Xerox, Figure 32. Others reverse gradually, with less spectacular volume, like Du Pont, Figure 27.

Sometimes an uncharacteristic and sustained burst of volume indicates a fundamental change in the prospects of a company, a merger in the works, a big news story soon to break. Be alert for unusual volume, a stock appearing on the most active list suddenly, or one making new highs several days in a row.

If an uptrend has been in progress for four or five days with an accelerating upward movement of the accumulation/distribution index, you should *not* follow this move if the stock has made a 10 percent or greater appreciation, as the odds are against the move continuing. Note again, this is for short-term option trading.

The key is to get into the trend just as it develops with pinpoint timing, near the edge-band of the envelope if possible. Usually if you get in too late there is not enough time or distance for price action left within the stock's envelope to make a profitable option trade. Exceptions do occur at major overall market reversal points, providing moves of 15 to 20 percent or more, but this is rare. If you are not in at the beginning of a move, do not try to chase it—many times you will be wrong and will be whipsawed in short order.

The most effective and safest time to take a call option position is when a downward move of at least 10 percent has just been completed. When it is accompanied by several days of distribution in the accumulation/distribution line and the line is slowing down on a day-to-day basis, or when the line has made a bottom within the last two days, you may feel confident that it is time to buy. This is the action point for trend reversal for which you are searching.

Remember to watch for *divergence* between the stock price line and the accumulation/distribution line. This occurs with the Stewart formula, just as it does with the Williams. See Figure 16 and accompanying text. Divergence is a strong signal and has predictive value.

The accumulation/distribution index gives you a very effective tool for helping your thinking and decision-making *when accompanied by other checkpoints in the system*. The accumulation/distribution lines are shown plotted and explained on individual stocks in Chapter 16.

ELEVEN

Analysis of the
Dow Jones Industrials

The most important question to answer before trading a stock or option is, what is the technical condition of the overall market and where is it headed? Or, what time is it on the stock market clock? As previously stated, 9 times out of 10 you must be in phase with the overall market movement of the Dow Jones Industrials or the Standard & Poor's 500 Average to be successful in short- or intermediate-term trading.

As outlined in Chapter 9, I prefer to use Lloyd's Moving Balance Indicator for measuring the buying and selling pressure and momentum of the overall market, since this composite indicator includes both advancing volume and advance/decline figures for the total New York Stock Exchange.

Figure 19 shows a one year history of the Dow Jones Industrial Average and the Moving Balance Indicator. You can see that approximately twenty significant reversal points occurred during these twelve months from September 1, 1978, until August 31, 1979. For market-timing purposes then, you were given 10 ideal places to buy and 10 to sell if you took action at these MBI bottoms and tops. Had you referred only to this indicator, how good would your predictions of movement of the Dow Jones Indsutrial Average have been?

Table 13 accompanying Figure 19 gives a 12-month summary of the Dow Jones movement and shows that you could have ideally predicted a total of about 805 Dow points during this time period. Note the range included plus 395 points and minus 410 points, and that the market went up just about as much as down. It is also interesting to point out

95

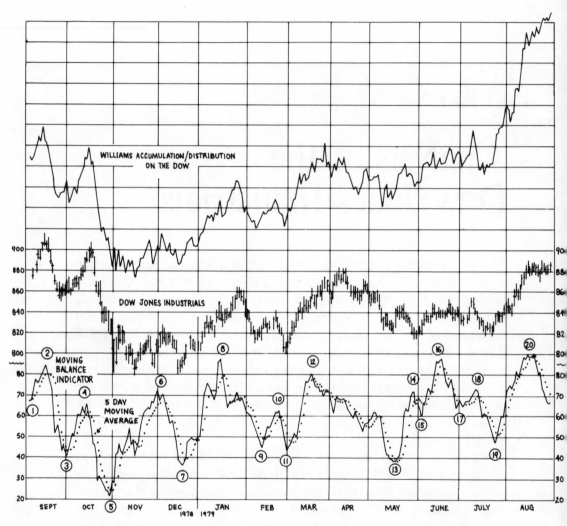

Figure 19. Dow Jones Industrial Average and Williams' Accumulation/Distribution, combined wth MBI.

TABLE 13 Dow Points Between MBI Reversals with Number of Trading Days in Each Move

MBI Reversal Points	Time Between Reversal Points (days)	Change in Dow Points
1–2	7	+ 25
2–3	8	− 50
3–4	10	+ 40
4–5	12	−130
5–6	30	+ 20
6–7	15	− 40
7–8	20	+ 70
8–9	22	− 40
9–10	9	+ 30
10–11	7	− 40
11–12	13	+ 60
12–13	45	− 40
13–14	8	+ 30
14–15	5	− 30
15–16	12	+ 30
16–17	14	− 10
17–18	12	+ 20
18–19	10	− 30
19–20	22	+ 70
	14.7 days average	805 total points

that the market was essentially unchanged at the end of this 12-month period, but there were good swings during the twelve month period even in a neutral trending market environment.

The average movement of each swing was about 40 points, or 5 percent of the Dow Jones Industrial Average. *A 5 percent move* in the average can coincide with *a 10 percent move* in an individual stock that has a Beta factor (see Glossary) of 2.0 or higher. While these Dow trends were in effect, one could find many examples of accompanying stock options that doubled in value during these market swings.

Also observe that the average time the trend remained intact was about three weeks, which is adequate time for a complete option trade. During some time periods, these trends continue as long as six weeks, but some short-term movements last for only two weeks, which means you must always be on guard to spot trend reversals. You sometimes get an interruption in the Moving Balance Indicator occurring before a significant top or bottom in the market average, but this does not happen often. Occasionally you must take a smaller profit by closing an option position early since the trend has a few more days to go before actually changing direction. However, there is an old and true adage that states it is always better to sell a little too soon than too late.

A further study of the Moving Balance Indicator in relation to the Dow Industrials shows that bottoms are much more definitive and better timed than tops. This can be seen by looking at the MBI reversal points which coincide closely with short-term bottoms in the Dow. However, the MBI usually peaks out *before* the market tops in most cases. This is to your advantage, if you think about it—a well-defined bottom reversal to buy into, a few days warning on the tops.

The top line of the graph in Figure 19 is a line I have called the Wiliams' Accumulation/Distribution on the Dow Jones Industrial Average. This index is calculated by using Larry Williams' formula:

$$\frac{\text{close} - \text{open}}{\text{high} - \text{low}} \times \text{volume} = +/- \text{ figure}$$

The figures for the Dow Jones Industrial Average are found inside the back page of the *Wall Street Journal*. They are calculated each day, and the resulting plus or minus figure is plotted cumulatively to make a continuous line. Determine whether the figure is a plus or a minus this way: If the close was lower than the open, the result is plotted as a *minus* figure and is *subtracted* from the cumulative line. If the close was *higher* than the open, the result is plotted as a *plus* figure and is *added* to the cumulative line. In other words, this is the same calculation that Williams used in his calculations for the accumulation/distribution of an individual stock. To my knowledge, Williams does not use this calculation for the Dow Jones Industrial Average itself. I plot it to see whether or not the buying or selling pressure coincides with or diverges from the movement of the Dow and use it as another short-term indicator.

An example of how a *minus* day is calculated (close is lower than open):

Date	Open	High	Low	Close	(000) Volume	Williams Accumulation/ Distribution
8/31	885.41	889.68	881.40	884.64	2363	−219.7

Close minus open is: $884.64 - 885.41 = -0.77$
High minus low is: $889.68 - 881.40 = 8.28$

$$\frac{close - open}{high - low} = -0.77 \div 8.24 = -0.0934$$

$$0.0934 \text{ times } 2362 \text{ (volume)} = -219.7$$

A *plus* figure is plotted when the *close* is higher than the *open*.

Usually, the Williams accumulation/distribution line moves with the Dow through its trends and cycles, its patterns closely duplicating what is happening in the Dow. When the direction of this line is in phase with the Moving Balance Indicator, you have another confirming trend indicator for the Dow. In some instances, accumulation will continue to be seen after the MBI has indicated a top. This sometimes allows you to stay in positions a few days longer, until the market accumulation phase tops out—final confirmation that the move is over for the short-term.

Special note: There is an important phenomenon that may be observed in the MBI during extremely strong bull market moves that you should be aware of. When the market takes off on a prolonged buying spree that lasts for an unusually long time, the following conditions may exist: there may be a succession of many massive-volume days, the Dow and other market indexes seem to be going straight up without hesitation, the accumulation/distribution line on the Dow is going straight up, and the MBI will go into an oscillating mode in overbought territory. Do not be fooled into selling by apparent MBI top reversals that last for only a few days, go down slightly for a few days (but not very convincingly), and then go up again. During a very strong, prolonged upmove, the MBI can oscillate like this within a narrow range so long as the market is continuing its strong uptrend. The key things to watch for during these unusual periods are: trend-channel breaks in the Dow and individual stocks and—most important—a definite break or rounding top in the accumulation/distribution line on the Dow. You will know you have a *real* reversal in the MBI *when it is accompanied by a break in the trend-channel on the Dow and the Dow accumulation/distribution line.* Never become so enamoured with *one* indicator that you fail to see a contradiction in another. Always look for confirmation in as many indicators as possible.

This cautionary note applies in reverse in sharply falling bear markets as well. Do not be fooled by an MBI that is oscillating in oversold territory and giving weak buy signals if the Dow and its accumulation/distribution line show continuing weakness and there has been no decisive breakout on the upside.

Occasionally, divergence occurs (see Dow Chart, Figure 19), as in the period from late November, 1978 through August, 1979, when heavy accumulation was present. The Dow itself did not indicate such strength. In fact, the Dow remained essentially neutral throughout most of the period, confined within a trading range between 800–900, while its accumulation/distribution line was in a strong uptrend from November 1978 onward. This overall long-term accumulation predicted the strong upward movement in the Dow stocks starting in the latter part of July 1979, and continuing through August, September, and into October. In other words, the Dow stocks were *under net accumulation,* and not distribution during the one year period shown.

After you have worked with these indicators for a period of time you will develop a feel for the overall condition and direction of the market. You will then be able to determine whether the market is developing oversold or overbought conditions within itself, and these measurements will improve your timing for taking option positions. As I have pointed out, you need to make these calculations and plot them so that you can get into the market ahead of the crowd. Your data need to be up to date on a daily basis. It simply takes too much time for advisory services to mail information to you on optimum buy and sell points. You must develop the ability to form an opinion daily on the internal strength or weakness of the overall market. This background allows you to project the most likely movement of the average during the next two to three weeks or 15 market days, and that is the average time frame for round trip option trading.

TWELVE

Selecting Stocks for Charting, Tracking, and Trading

As stated earlier in the text, it is desirable to keep up daily with a few of the major stocks that have underlying options. These are the stocks for which you should plot the accumulation/distribution index, and you should study them more closely for cyclic action.

LEARN TO THINK IN PERCENTAGE MOVES

There are several criteria in selecting the stocks that you plan to keep up with continuously as you watch for reversal points. First, the companies selected should be large leading industrial stocks, preferably in the $40 to $100 price range. When these stocks are chosen you can be assured of a large following and a liquid market in both call and put options. They will track well, and will usually provide the 10 to 15 percent moves you are looking for. Low-priced stocks for option trading should be avoided because:

1. Low-priced stocks rarely move enough to make profitable trades.
2. A 10 percent move on a $10 stock is $1 in intrinsic value, while a ten percent move on a $50 stock is $5 in intrinsic value. In-the-money options will move up dollar for dollar the same amount

101

that the underlying stock moves, once the stock price has reached *parity* (which is the point at which the current stock price equals the striking price plus the time value part of the premium).

3. The cost of the option is about the same, but the difference in profit potential is considerable, as the following Table 14 shows:

TABLE 14   Comparison of Option Trades in a $20 Stock and a $50 Stock

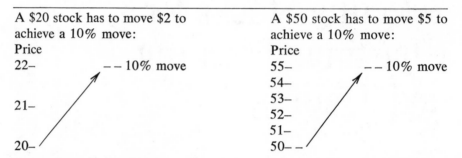

A $20 stock has to move $2 to achieve a 10% move:	A $50 stock has to move $5 to achieve a 10% move:
Price	Price
22– – – 10% move	55– – – 10% move
	54–
	53–
21–	52–
	51–
20–	50– –

Assumptions: A 10 percent move is expected in each stock. A purchase is made of a $5 in-the-money option with 60–90 days life in it. (All values are approximate.) The stocks are currently selling at:

$20	$50
Buy a March 15 call at 5½.	Buy a March 45 call at 6½.
Stock moves to $22, a 10% move.	Stock moves to $55, a 10% move.
Option goes to about 7¼.	Option goes to about 10¾.
(Time premium shrinks a little.)	(Time premium shrinks a little.)
Sell option for an approximate profit of $200.	Sell option for an approximate profit of $400.

As you can see from the above example, the higher priced stock provides twice the profit potential as the lower priced one.

Another thing to watch is *chart scale*. Since chart services must maintain the same size and time frame for every stock they plot, you will find great distortions in the appearance of the moves. A $10 stock must fill up the same amount of chart space that a $100 stock does. The $10 stock will have such an expanded scale that it will look like it is really swinging and making some fantastic moves, when in reality all the activity takes place between $10 and $12!

An $80 stock may be scaled $10 to one line space, and show very little movement on the chart. With a change of scale the cycles and swings become much more apparent. This is a good reason for charting some of your own stocks. You will soon be able to mentally adjust for scale. Remember, learn to think in *percentage* moves rather than in *dollar* moves.

IDENTIFYING CYCLIC CHARACTERISTICS

In addition, while scanning an up-to-date stock chart for at least twelve months, look for dominant cyclic characteristics. This means when you draw the envelope boundary of the intermediate term you get a picture of the smooth, flowing motion of the stock as it moves from the lower to the upper edge-band and back (oversold to overbought). Some stocks work much better from a cyclic standpoint than others, and this can be seen by looking at their history. Remember, for short-term option trading it is not necessary to have extremely large upward or downward stock movement since you are only looking for changes that produce a 10 to 15 percent price change. Look for stocks that swing rhythmically, and that offer six to eight trading opportunities per year. They will track well.

After you have drawn in your envelope boundaries, look for edge-band reversals that are somewhat periodic. When you find a stock with such periodic reversals in its past, you have a way to estimate probable future reversal points and the prices at which they are most likely to occur.

VOLATILITY

Another factor to consider while screening stocks for option trading is *volatility,* which is a measure of how rapidly and how far a stock is likely to move based on recent past trading action. Volatility can be gauged in a number of ways.

Capitalization, the total number of shares available for trading, tells you something about volatility. A stock with a very small capitalization will be extremely volatile when it moves because when demand develops fewer shares are available for sale and prices can soar dramatically. Conversely, if selling develops, supply will tend to make it drop just as rapidly. In trading stocks this can be a plus factor, if you are nimble enough.

For the purposes of short-term option trading, however, *small* capitalization is not an important factor. Most of the leading option stocks are highly capitalized to assure broad interest and liquidity to both the stock and options. Large volume is necessary to make significant price changes in these stocks.

Another way to measure volatility in a stock is by its *Beta factor*. This term describes how the stock moves in relation to a general market move. A very high Beta of 2.0, for example, means the stock is twice as volatile as the market on the average. A Beta of 1.0 means the stock moves normally, just as the market moves. Obviously, you should not track a stock individually on a daily basis if the Beta factor is very low (less than 1.0), as you must get better price swings than that in order to make money with put and call options.

Daily Graphs Stock Option Guide publishes the Beta, and bases theirs on the past five years.

When relying on published material, be sure you know what is measured in a Beta factor—what the time span is, how often calculated, when published, how old the data is. Many advisory services and stock chart books print the Beta factor among the statistics they provide for investors, but their Betas often vary. If you discover the Beta is radically different for the same stock in two different services, check the "explanation of terms" in the front or back of the book to see how each Beta is calculated.

Keep in mind that the Beta is constantly changing according to the stock's recent short-term volatility. A stock that has been trading flat, or in a very narrow range for some time may have a very *negative* published Beta, like 0.98 (comparing it with the overall market), but a *recent* surge in price and volume and subsequent widening of the trading range will mean a new Beta factor is in effect. If you could calculate it yourself you would have information not yet available through the published services.

The message here is, do not rule out a stock for trading purposes based on published Beta alone—look at the recent action. A breakout from a trading range with high volume is a good sign you can forget the Beta in this instance.

A high and rising *short interest* adds to volatility. The trouble with short interest figures as a predictor of near-term moves is that they are always published a month late. By the time you get them the real short interest in a stock may have changed drastically. There is no certain way to know when a stock is being sold short, or when short positions are being covered.

It is expected that when a stock with a high short interest begins to move up the shorts will rush to cover, thus fueling the rally, tripping stop loss orders along the way. Don't rely solely on short interest to indicate direction, although there is no doubt it does make a stock more volatile, especially on upside chart breakouts.

SELECTING STOCKS FOR DAILY CHARTING

Ideally, it would be great to have the accumulation/distribution index for all stocks on which listed options are available. This is impractical, however. You should not try to track or plot more than 15 or so issues on a daily basis. This work will take 15 minutes per day when you get it down to a mechanical routine, and should be kept up on a day-to-day basis, if possible. The reason it should be done daily is that action signals are given at any time on any day during the week, and you will want to spot the trend change and accumulation/distribution reversals as soon as they occur, before the prices are apparent on most published chart services. Remember, you are looking for all of the advantages you can get on precision timing to improve your odds in trading the stock options. You can get in a position three to four days before it becomes apparent to other traders that a trend is reversing. The daily plotting of a few key stocks also helps in developing a feel for the overall market in terms of buying or selling pressure.

It is a good idea to have a variety of industries represented in your selection. The stocks in an industry tend to move together and you do not want all of your charts doing the same thing at the same time.

Note that a signal in a particular stock often gives a signal for the *industry* as well—if you chart an oil company, for instance, and get an early signal, quickly check the other oils. A more advantageous option might be apparent. If you see activity in an auto stock, check the others, and so on. This is particularly true if there is a more volatile industry-related stock available for option trading.

It is good to select some stocks that have *puts* available so that you can participate in the down moves as well. Often, after you have completed a successful call option trade, you will find the stock giving an ideal *put* signal, giving you the opportunity to make another profit immediately. You may wonder why I don't advocate just "shorting" calls instead of buying puts. There is less risk in puts, and one does not have to put up any money to cover the short position. Therefore, to keep things as simple as possible, and eliminate unnecessary risks, I limit my option trading as well as the scope of this book to the buying of calls and puts only, and selling these long positions to close the trades.

There are, of course, many exotic and complicated ways to use puts and calls, involving multiples, simultaneous and sequential contracts, as well as writing calls on stocks held long, writing naked calls and puts, and so on. I do not involve myself in those, because I do not believe anything beats a simple, direct, easy-to-follow method—especially for someone who has a full-time career.

While screening stocks for good option trading candidates, be sure to look for stocks that make at least seven or eight good moves a year, if you plan to go to the trouble of plotting them daily. You want ones that will give you enough swing signals to make all of your work pay off.

Most likely the stocks that you stay with for plotting and tracking daily will develop major cyclic turning points over a period of months. Many times they will be uninteresting to you, especially if they are in a prolonged period of base-building, or if no particular trend can be identified. This cannot be helped, however, and usually you will find at least one to three issues out of fifteen that give a stronger signal than the remaining ones, which you will ignore. It is frustrating, however, to plot a stock for a period of twelve months and never attempt to trade a put or call, since it never appeared positive or interesting enough for you to take a position. This must occur in order to help make up your mind on more promising opportunities by a comparative method. You may decide from time to time to "weed out" the disappointing ones, and pick up a few new ones.

SUMMARY OF IMPORTANT POINTS FOR SELECTING STOCKS FOR DAILY CHARTING

1. Look for moves of 10 to 15 percent.
2. Choose stocks in the $40 to $100 range.
3. Look for frequent periodic cycles.
4. Look for six to eight trading opportunities per year, and pick the ones that "swing."
5. Check volatility factors such as Beta, capitalization, and short interest.
6. Select some that have puts to take advantage of the down moves.
7. Select a group that represents a variety of industries.

SCANNING A CHART SERVICE FOR ADDITIONAL TRADING OPPORTUNITIES

It is important that you have a weekly chart service, such as *Daily Graphs Stock Option Guide,* to keep you up to date on all listed option stocks, as well as the progress of the market itself.

As you scan each weekly issue, you will be attracted to stocks you are not plotting, because you have about three hundred choices versus the fifteen you are tracking daily. (There may be additional stocks in which options will become available from time to time.) From the option guide scan you can reduce your choices to about ten of the three hundred stocks for closer study. You may think scanning three hundred stocks every Monday is too great a task. Not so. Soon you will know which ones to skip—the low-priced ones, the ones in flat trading patterns, the ones in strong downtrends that do not have puts, ones that move slowly and do not swing in short-term moves. The utilities rarely offer much action. You will develop favorites which you intuitively know are ready to move. You will develop an eye for spotting signals like breakouts, consolidations, increased volume, or a previously dormant stock that is showing signs of life.

In a scan this large, you are going to spot some promising potential trades. There are several factors you can concentrate on, even though you do not have an accumulation/distribution index. You can do the following to test whether you have the basis for a good trade:

1.   Construct the constant-width envelope for the past twelve months, notice the reversal points, and lead it out into the time zone two to three weeks beyond the plotted data.

2.   Draw a mid-band dotted line down the center of this envelope and observe the curve shape. This line will closely approximate the 50 day moving average line with a 25 day lag.

3.   Look at the volume characteristics of the stock and consolidation zones.

4.   After you have an envelope on the trading, determine if the stock is at or near an edge-band which should be its reversal point. If you have a rapidly rising upward envelope and your other market timing indicators say "go," you have a sound situation.

5.   Determine mentally where the expected short-term cycle point should turn, at what price, and what time.

6.   Look at the relative strength of the stock as listed. Is it stronger than the market? Has the activity of trading as shown by the volume during the past several weeks been higher than usual? All of these factors must be in phase before you buy an option.

With the Moving Balance Indicator and the Williams Accumulation/Distribution on the Dow Averages themselves in phase, and using the above test, you can greatly increase your odds for a successful trade, even though you are not plotting these stocks daily with accumulation/distribution. In summary, what you are looking for in this scanning selection are strong, interesting chart patterns. You want stocks that move 10 to 15 percent short term, preferably in the $40 to $100 price range. Look for strong uptrends with short-term swings. Watch for stocks with recent increases in volume. These particular stocks make good selections because trading interest temporarily tends to increase their volatility. Some strong moves can come from this activity. When compared to the stock's normal trading pattern the relative volume and resulting price action are helpful in picking out a stock that can move much more rapidly than usual.

You do not have to be in on the ground floor on all of these patterns. Some of the major cyclic reversals may already be three to four months along the way, but still have potential to go much higher. When you time your entry properly, using the techniques described, you are sometimes buying high and expecting to sell higher, and this is exactly what can be done in many cases where positions are taken during strong continuing patterns. These are dynamic positions to be in, and these stocks always jump out of the chart scan by showing rapidly increasing relative strength and smooth upward biased envelope trading patterns.

PART THREE

The Stewart System Puts It All Together: Checklists, Forms to Use, Rules to Obey, Lessons In Charting and Analyzing Trades, Self-Appraisal, and Getting You Started Trading Options

After acquiring a considerable amount of knowledge about market psychology, market cycles, market indicators, and delving thoroughly into technical analysis for individual stocks, I found that I had to develop a simple way to combine it all into one system—a system that could be followed *mechanically,* take a minimum amount of time, and make the reasons for my trading decisions absolutely clear. I had to have reasons for buying, an expectation of what the ensuing move was likely to be, and a predetermined way to get out of the trade with the maximum profit. I needed a quick way to get out of the trade with the minimum loss if the trade did not develop as I had anticipated.

In working with the technical tools presented in Part Two, I found that certain things seemed to happen over and over again as I watched trades develop. Sometimes they happened in sequence, and sometimes they happened at the same time. Sometimes factors predicted future action. I discovered that some factors *always* seemed to be present when a successful trade was initiated, and that some things were the "kiss of death" to such a trade.

111

In order to organize these factors to anticipate the probable outcome of a trade, I began keeping checklists and utilizing a standard form for recording the data about each trade.

I have developed a list of 30 general rules for myself that encompass all the aspects covered in this book. It is helpful to review these rules (and to keep them constantly in mind) as each trade is initiated, as it progresses, and as it is finally concluded. Part Three presents them in final form. If you follow these rules scrupulously you will begin to see a marked improvement in your trading skills.

In Chapter 16, I bring the Stewart System together for you, and present a selection of stock charts that I kept on a daily basis during a year's time. I have included the techniques of chart analysis that I have found to be of most help, as well as some practical tips on the mechanics of charting stocks learned through trial and error, which may be of some help to you. I have combined the stock price action, the Stewart Accumulation/Distribution Index for the stock, and the MBI on one chart so you can see how they work together and can practice with them. I have explained how I interpret the charts, get signals and confirmations, detect divergence, and establish probable limits of potential trades. This is where the "art" comes in. As I said earlier in this book, interpretation is an individual thing. Each of us must develop his own way to interpret such data.

The charts selected for Chapter 16 are not all super trading stocks, nor are they all ones that had a great number of profitable trades during the time span covered. That would have given you unrealistic expectations, and I don't intend to exaggerate or deceive you into thinking you can simply select a group of stocks that will perform as you wish them to. The stock charts included are selected to give you an idea of the range of the different kinds of stocks you might select, to show you that some you follow will not live up to your expectations, that some will surprise you and become favorites, and that some will give you problems with chart scale, splits, or no action you can safely trade.

In Chapter 17 I describe what I believe typifies a successful option trader. As you may recall from the beginning of the book, I list the character traits of a layman who wants to be a successful speculator in options, to see if I (or you) had the psychological makeup to compete in this fast-paced area of the equity market. Now, after taking you through the Stewart System, I describe the qualities I think a *professional* trader must have so we can try to think and trade like a "pro."

Chapter 18 asks you the question again—are you cut out to be a speculator? This is the bottom line. If you feel you are, are you willing to give it your all, do your homework, and try to trade like a pro? If so, and you want to give it a try, I present some suggestions for developing your own plan of action and getting started trading options.

THIRTEEN

Master Checklist
for Buying Options

There are many factors that determine whether an option trade will turn out successfully, and all of these things have been mentioned and emphasized repeatedly. Now it is necessary to organize them in such a way that the decision-making process becomes *mechanical*. This will eliminate doubt, confusion, and the need to remember everything at once.

We need to measure all the parameters we can before we take an option position. The best way to do this is to make a checklist, organized in step-by-step sequence (sort of a "go-or-*no*-go" method, like the ones used for space shots!). Using this format, first make decisions about market conditions and the timing of the expected overall market move. Then check what the analysis of your individual stock chart is telling you about probable future action. (Remember, we are concerned with the very near term for these option positions.) If all signals are still "go," consult your Stock Option Guide (or similar publication) for help in deciding which option to buy. By the time you arrive at the end of the checklist, you should have the decision made, and it will only remain for you to take appropriate action.

Note: It is important to mention here that the *five to 15 days* I refer to so often in this book represents the most profitable period following a buy signal. Most of my successful trades have been of this duration. I do not mean to infer that all option trades have a time limit of 15 days. This is the *average* length of time the market takes to complete one-half of a short-term market cycle. (See the table following Figure 19 in Chapter

11.) The short-term cycle on which I base my work usually lasts from two to six weeks. That is five to 15 days on the upside and five to 15 days on the downside. Longer cycles do occur, and occasional strong continuing moves defy the short cycle. Special situations can cause a stock's price to override the expected cycle length. I do not advocate getting out of a profitable position just because fifteen market days have gone by. *Stay* in a winning position until the trendline breaks—let your profits run!

TAKING A LONG CALL POSITION

From Your Dow, Williams Accumulation/Distribution, MBI Chart

(1)   Does the intermediate envelope boundary of the Dow Jones Industrial Average indicate a reversal from the lower edge-band is beginning, with the potential for an up move of at least 5 percent or 40 Dow points? During the 1978–1979 time period, the Dow was in the 800 range, and the usual moves were about 5–6 percent between reversals. For examples, see points 5, 7, 11, 13, and 19 on the Dow/MBI Chart (Figure 19).

(2)   Has the MBI completed a cycle of the approximate duration of recent past cycles? Is the MBI making a bottom reversal after a recent decline? (Ten to twenty days of declining is common before reversal takes place.) Is the MBI in the range where it has frequently reversed before? (Longer than usual cycles tend to bottom much lower, and usually indicate *major* cycle bottoms. Shorter than usual cycles tend to reverse at higher values.)

(3)   Has the 5 day moving average of the MBI started to flatten out or show that it is slowing down, as it must do before reversing and turning up?

(4)   Is the Williams Accumulation/Distribution on the Dow showing a bottom or a two to three day reversal pattern indicating that accumulation is taking over from distribution?

(5)   Has the overall market been going down in a trend channel for at least the last 10–20 days, and is there an indication of a trendline break to the upside, suggesting a reversal is occurring?

From the Individual Stock Chart

(6) What does the intermediate cycle envelope suggest for the stock in question? Call option purchases are usually most successful when this envelope is trending upward or sideways. If the envelope slants downward, you will only be trying to trade a small upward movement or a technical rebound in a downtrend. This *can* be done with this system, but technical rebounds produce less profit with more risk because the moves are over so quickly. (Purchasing a put in a downtrending stock would make a lot more sense.) For examples of profitable technical rebounds in a falling stock, see Figure 25, Corning Glass, in early October and early November, 1978.

(7) Are you at a cycle point in the stock where you expect a trend break on the upside to occur according to your visual predictions for a reversal?

(8) Has your stock recently declined 8–10 percent along with the immediate past action of the market itself? *Note the exceptions:* When the general market is in a strongly rising uptrend, and a cyclic pullback is expected, there will occasionally be a very small decline, or in some cases, none at all. Sometimes the market will just consolidate in a tight sideways pattern for some days and then continue the strong upward move. (See the December 1978–January 1979 move in the Dow and MBI, Figure 19, and Xerox, Figure 32). The same can be seen in reverse in sharply falling markets. If your MBI, Accumulation/Distribution Index and other factors are favorable, an 8–12 percent decline before taking a position can be disregarded in this case because you obviously have a very strong uptrend going. Look for chart patterns like flags, pennants, and triangles that predict these measured moves. Be prepared to close the position quickly if it does not break out of the consolidation on the upside promptly.

(9) Has the Stewart Accumulation/Distribution Index stopped going down and started to go sideways? Is it accumulating on the upside after several days of selling pressure? This indicates that the stock is in a technically oversold condition and is ready for an upward rebound.

(10) Based on your analysis of the constant-width envelope you have drawn for the stock and recent short-term cycles, can you make a prediction that the stock is likely to move to the upper edge-band in the next

few weeks? Is there potential for at least a fifty percent move in the option you will select?

(11)   Does past history, three to twelve months, show a heavy overhead resistance zone that will take very large trading volume to penetrate? If so, expect this zone to be your short-term objective, as that is where you would expect the stock to slow down, move sideways, or reverse as heavy selling comes in.

(12   Does the stock have a long-term cycle pattern that you can get a mental picture of to reinforce your buying decision? This is *very important* and helps you to be sure you have the overall long-term picture clearly in mind.

(13)   In the past, once a trend starts, has the stock moved 3, 5, or 7 points before reversing? If so, this is normally the movement you expect for a trade this time. If it appears that a longer-term cyclic low point is occurring in the stock, you can get a larger than predicted upward movement. This occurs only at major trend reversal points where other longer-term cycles are reinforcing the moves at the same time. You do not usually study this phenomenon for short-term option trades.

(14)   Is the stock in a tight trading zone, rectangular box, ascending triangle, symmetrical triangle, or other significant pattern? The Accumulation/Distribution Index helps to resolve the direction of the breakout many times by showing early divergence from the stock price line. You should only take a position during or after the first day you see a breakout occur.

From Your Stock Option Guide

(15)   Does the option have at least 20 to 60 days of life in it, and is it above the striking price? (See 16 below.) If you are trading very close to date of expiration, the time premium will deteriorate very rapidly, and unless your option is in-the-money and you get an immediate and spectacular move, you will lose all of your capital. It is interesting to note on a stock chart how often a sharp drop in price occurs in the last few days of an option's life.

(16)   Is the option at or above the striking price? It is better to trade in options that have some intrinsic value. The options that have more time and that are deeper in-the-money, above the striking price, are always safer to trade than are ones close to expiration or out-of-the-money.

It is always better to have some insurance that if your decision is wrong, especially in the short term, you can sell your position and still retain most of your capital.

(17)   Does the option have a fair premium? This should be checked for theoretical value as shown weekly in the *Daily Graphs Stock Option Guide*. The theoretical value is a calculated value that includes both intrinsic and time components. Volatile and active high-priced issues sometimes carry very high premiums, and this should be taken into consideration. Sometimes you can locate undervalued options from these tables which will help you determine if you are paying too much premium based on the stock price, the striking price, the volatility, and the time to option expiration.

USING THE OPTION TRADING CHECKLIST AND TRANSACTION HISTORY

After the above questions have been answered, I find it helpful to use the following option trading checklist and transaction history. This makes certain you have answered the major questions before buying an option and is another form of the mental discipline you should use on a mechanical and logical basis before committing money in the options market. This may seem unnecessary and time-consuming, as most of us like to make immediate decisions and "shoot from the hip," being very enthusiastic at the time of purchase. I can assure you, if you slow down enough to think to make sure you have positive answers as outlined in the checklist, you will do a better job of timing option purchases, and, therefore, have a much better chance of making correct buying decisions which will lead to profitable trades. It will also provide you with a written record of your trade to analyze later for improving technique, seeing where you went wrong, and so on.

The hard facts of the above decision-making process replace all of the rumors, earnings projections, recommendations from advisory services and other material. The beauty of this is that you can determine them for yourself and, therefore, draw your own conclusions about a trading possibility without distortion or confusion from other input. This is the single most important discipline you can develop. You must learn to work and think for yourself if you are going to be a successful option trader.

Option Trading Check List and Transaction History

Call Options

Company Name and Stock Symbol _____ Price _____

Option Symbol _____ Price _____ Expiration Month _____

Date Purchased _____ Price _____ Number of Options _____

Technical Indicators at Purchase

MBI Value _____ Trend _____ Date of Bottom _____ Value _____

MBI Weeks From Last Bottom _____

Stewart Acc/Dis on Stock _____ Trend_____

Channel Trend Break Price _____

Recent Top Price _____ Date _____ % Down _____

Intermediate Cycle: Up _____ Down _____

Intermediate Cycle Boundary: Lower _____ Upper _____

Short Cycle: Expected Top   Date _____ Price _____

　　　　　　　 Expected Bottom   Date _____ Price _____

Special Chart Pattern (Description) _____

_____

_____

50-Day Moving Average Price of Stock: Up _____ Down _____ Neutral _____

Dow-Williams Acc/Dis   Positive _____ Negative _____

Date Option Sold _____ Price _____ Stock Price _____

Description of MBI: Value _____ 3-Day Top Indicated _____

Stewart Acc/Dis on Stock _____

Comments on Trade _____

_____

_____

_____

120

BUYING PUTS

Put positions for expected stock declines are taken just at the opposite ends of the spectrum from call options. Because this is true, the technical work done on the market or individual stocks is used to establish these positions just as easily as for call positions. Just get your checklist to work in reverse and you have the answers for a put. It is important to learn to trade puts as well as calls, because a downtrending stock provides the same profit opportunities that an uptrending stock provides for calls. In a neutral-trending market, the short-term *down* moves are almost equal to the *up* moves. By using puts you can be in the market a greater percent of the total available time. Actually, with some study, the downtrends are as easy to identify as the uptrends. Frequently you will find after completing a successful call trade your work is signalling a *put,* and your homework is already done!

Even after you have done all of the work, you will find the buying decision is usually much easier than the selling decision, whether you are taking a profit or cutting a loss short. The next chapter will cover the intricacies of closing out a trade.

FOURTEEN

Master Checklist
for Selling Options

It is human nature to procrastinate, to wait and see, to change the game plan as you go along. Nowhere else will you find this attitude as disastrous to follow as in the trading of options. Selling a position, whether it is to realize a gain or to cut a loss short, is much harder to accomplish successfully and takes 10 times more discipline than buying does.

When buying a option or a stock we are always enthusiastic about the outlook for appreciation. If we see that we have a good gain, we always want more. We don't want to leave any additional profit on the table. (How many times have you been greedy, and tried to wait for just a little more profit, only to see the stock quickly reverse, wiping out your profits?)

Here are some things that happened to me before I started using my rules for getting out of a trade: I would take a position based on what I felt was a good buy signal (or sell signal for puts), and, after several days, when the expected action did not develop, I would tell myself, "Well, maybe I was just a little early—I'll just wait a little longer and see what happens." What usually happened was *nothing,* or the stock would go down, taking my option premium with it. Then I would tell myself, "Maybe it will move back up on the next cycle—there are (blank) number of weeks until expiration." The time premium would shrink, and now I would just think about waiting to break even. None of these things worked. If this sounds familiar to you it is probably because you have done the same things yourself, either with stocks or options. There is a big difference, though—a stock can be held indefinitely, and if you wait long enough, you can sometimes bail yourself out of a bad decision. Not so with options. There is no way to bail out—you are either right or wrong. Nine times out of 10 hope and procrastination cause losses to increase in trading options. I have run many of them to zero simply by hoping and waiting.

Determined that I was going to quit that nonsense, I developed a master checklist to use for selling decisions like the one I had made for buying decisions. I abide by it strictly, no matter what. I keep my Option Trading Checklist and Transaction History form handy so that I have it before me as a reminder, a record of what my goal or expectation on the trade was to be, and so that I cannot change the rules of the game once I am in a trade. I record how the transaction turns out—to keep me honest, and to study further for improved future trading results.

The main thing to keep in mind is that the market (or an individual stock) cares nothing for your predictions, your ego, or your emotions. The only thing that affects it is supply (distribution) and demand (accumulation). Nothing else determines the price movement.

SELLING: THE TOUGH DECISION

Most of the reasons for selling an option are just the opposite of the reasons listed in the master checklist for setting up a trade or taking a long position in a call. For selling a long call position, ask yourself the following questions:

From Your Dow, Williams Accumulation/Distribution, MBI Chart

(1)   Does the intermediate envelope boundary of the Dow Jones Industrial Average indicate a reversal is forming at the upper edge-band of its trading range with the likelihood of a down move of at least 5 percent or 40 Dow points? (See Figure 19.)

(2)   Has the MBI completed a cycle of the approximate duration of the recent past cycles? Is the MBI making a top reversal after a recent rally? Is the MBI in the range where it has frequently reversed before? (Remember longer than usual cycles tend to top out much higher, shorter than usual cycles tend to top out at lower values.)

(3)   Has the 5 day moving average of the MBI started to flatten out and go sideways, as it must do when it turns down?

(4)   Is the Williams Accumulation/Distribution Index on the Dow showing a top or a reversal pattern developing indicating that distribution is taking over? Watch for divergence.

(5)   Are the Dow Jones Industrial stocks showing an indication that the short-term trend is over either by churning, or by refusing to make progress? Has the average broken its uptrend? Has the average made its move to the envelope boundary you sketched in?

From the Individual Stock Chart

(6)   Has the stock moved to the point you projected near the upper edge-band of the intermediate-term envelope?

(7)   Are you at a cycle point in the stock where you would expect a trend-break to the downside to occur?

(8)   Is there evidence that the accumulation/distribution line is starting to drop while the price action line moves sideways or up? When you see such divergence it is a warning that the move is exhausting itself.

(9)   Has your stock recently rallied 8–10 percent along with the market itself? It may be time to take your profits. (Exception: if the stock and its accumulation/distribution line continue to look strong, stay in the winning position until you get a trend-channel break or other sell signal. Watch for continuation patterns like flags, pennants, triangles, and so on, that sometimes suggest measured moves. Be prepared to close the position quickly, however, if a break to the downside out of the consolidation (continuation) pattern occurs.

(10)   Is the stock price moving into heavy congestion or a resistance zone that can be seen by studying its chart for the last 3 to 12 months?

(11)   Has the stock broken its short-term uptrend channel?

(12)   Has a new earnings report or other major news been published on the stock? At such times the stock can go up and churn on relatively higher volume and this is usually a very good sell point if the news is favorable.

(13)   Is the option getting close to its expiration date? Don't wait until the last few days of an option's life to close it out. All too often the stock will drop right before expiration date, leaving you holding a worthless option.

SELLING PUT OPTIONS

Again, as in the checklist for buying options, to know when to sell a put option you must get your *selling checklist* to work in reverse. It might be pointed out that here the very reasons you would buy a *call* (see the checklist for buying calls) would be your reasons for closing out a put position. To put it another way, when all the market conditions and your stock analysis says it is time to buy a call you can be sure it is time to close your put position!

STOPPING LOSSES

Remember, this system is a *short-term* trading method, with expected market moves to be completed in a relatively short period of time.

No one goes into a long call position expecting to take a loss, but losses will occur on about 20 to 30 percent of your choices, since it is not possible to make accurate predictions 100 percent of the time; 60 to 80 percent accuracy is the most you can expect by any method.

My number one rule for preserving capital is, if the stock and the option have not moved in the direction you projected within five days after taking the position, *close it out at the market*. I cannot emphasize the importance of this rule enough. If exercised, it will allow you to retain most of your working capital and free both your capital and your decision-making capability for studying the next move. It is always better to trade five straight trades with a loss of 25 percent on each trade than to let one option position go to zero. You usually know when buying an option whether you are correct the first day you are in the position. In situations that you know are wrong, the sooner you admit it to yourself, and the quicker you go in and close or sell the option, the better off you will be. In nearly all cases where gains are made, the options move up rapidly during the first few days after they are purchased. This is the confirmation you want that the trend you have predicted is happening. You should not stand for more than a 30 percent loss in an option position—*sell it!*

Another important point to remember is never wait out another market cycle or Moving Balance Indicator cycle while in an open position. Over the longer term you may be exactly right in the movement of the stock only to see the option time premium deteriorate and produce a loss. Even if the stock and the option eventually go up, you may have only a small profit because of the time factor alone. Also, it is not good psychologically for a short-term trader to be in a long position when he sees the technical indicators pointing to a lower market, which tells him he should either be in puts, or a short position, or out of the market altogether. You do not have to take this added emotional strain for an undetermined period. Before the market goes into an oversold position and reverses to the upside, it will surely cost you, emotionally as well as financially.

These factors can be checked for any option and stock position you are in, and are the best guides I know of for making the sell decision. You must be able to reduce your decision making to a mechanical and technical system, with as little emotion as possible. Also, remember that the overall market seldom makes a 6 percent gain or loss, on the average, without a reversal or consolidation. This means that many high Beta stocks will make 10 percent or higher moves in the same time period, and this is about all you can predict for short-term option trading. If the movement has been greater than expected, but the rules tell you that all technical indications are in gear, you can stay in for a longer run until these conditions change. Again, this is done in a mechanical manner, and if done consistently will generate good gains in strong markets.

In summary, after proper timing is developed on buying, the next decision must be selling at the right time. If you can refer to and master the rules, you will continue to make gains in the option market on balance. The selling decision is the tough one, and always will be. You will never realize a profit until the option is sold, but losses are always there in a losing position.

FIFTEEN

Thirty Rules for Successful Trading

Experience in trading stock options has convinced me that a set of rules to serve as a guide to successful speculation is essential. I cannot emphasize enough the importance of making these rules an integral part of your decision making. If you follow them, they will keep you out of trouble as well as help you make proper decisions for successful option trading. Like a checklist, the more valid rules you can put down and follow the better are your chances of doing the right thing at the right time. It helps to remember that those who lose on balance are doing just the opposite, and this is the crowd from which you must separate yourself.

We all know that "rules are made to be broken," and certainly we all break them, or at least bend them at times. We must have the good judgment to know when it is appropriate to break or bend rules. The following guides will help you make such decisions:

- An exception applies—one that has proven to be true in the past more times than not.
- Some rules are absolutely *never* to be broken, and these you must recognize and always follow.
- When a few factors say "wait" or "no," but all the other applicable rules say "go," your instincts, based on past experience, will override your doubts. Be especially wary though, and be prepared to get out quickly if you are proven wrong.

129

The absolute rules are prefaced with "always" or "never." Rules that have special considerations are qualified. Your own experience will help you to add some of your own to this list.

(1) *Treat options as the speculative vehicle they are.* You should not think of them as investments. They are short-term speculations, unless you are a covered writer.

(2) *Always remember supply and demand are what make stock prices change.* Watch accumulation/distribution patterns for clues as to which way a stock might move. Watch the MBI for market reversals from overbought to oversold. Watch volume if you are not charting accumulation/distribution on a stock.

(3) *Always remember that options are short-lived instruments.* Correct timing is essential to success in option trading. If an option is at or below the striking price at expiration, your option will be worthless.

(4) *Consider one-half of your estimate for the length of the cycle you are trying to trade to be the maximum time you will be in the position.* With my system, most profitable trades are closed within fifteen market days. If profit doesn't start to build within five days, you have made a mistake.

(5) *Never take a position based on anyone's advice until you have done your own analysis.* Use the master checklist as a guide in determining whether the idea is sound. The same is true in selling out your position—sometimes brokers will encourage you to sell for a *small* profit when the timing is premature, thus diminishing your profit potential.

(6) *Stay out when confused or unsure of a situation.* It is much better to be in a cash position while you continue to search for a definite signal to act on. This frees your mind and calms your emotions for a correct decision.

(7) *Strive to be in when the action is taking place and out when you are uncertain about the technical conditions or overall direction.* Frequent trading and compounding is the best way to increase capital, but this does not mean you have to be 100 percent invested at all times.

(8) *Trade in stocks that show a predictable past pattern.* These are the stocks you can develop a feel for and better predict the trend for the next two or three weeks. It is amazing how history repeats itself in the stock market. Some stocks track much more predictably than others, which can be seen in scanning their charts.

(9) *Trade in high-priced, active issues.* Stocks in the $40 to $100

range have a wide following and there is liquidity in their options. Their cycles are more predictable, and the percentage moves greater than the low-priced stocks.

(10) *Think in percentage moves rather than dollar moves.* In selecting your stocks for option trading, pick ones that move 10–15 percent within their envelope boundaries.

(11) *Trade options which have intrinsic value (are in-the-money).* Such options should have 20 to 60 market days of life left. There is plenty of leverage in these options when you predict a 5 to 10 percent move in the stock within the next few weeks, and you have better downside protection if you are wrong and must close a position. This is not true if you are trading out-of-the-money options. An exception: occasionally it pays to make a short-term trade in an option slightly out-of-the-money, or at the striking price, when you are seeing *extremely strong accumulation* in a congestion zone and have at least 15 or 20 market days before expiration.

(12) *Watch the 50 day moving average.* It is safest to trade calls when this average is turning up, or already rising. When the average is turning down, or falling, it is safest to trade puts. When the average is neutral, or sideways, either calls or puts may be appropriate, but they must be watched more closely, and you must rely more heavily on other indicators.

(13) *Watch the 50 day moving average for confirmation that your envelope boundaries are correct.* The 50 day moving average, when shifted mentally one-half span (25 days) back in time (to the left), should form the same shape as the mid-band for your constant-width envelope.

(14) *Look for breakouts from congestion zones, and for other chart patterns you can identify.* Get into these movements quickly or leave them alone, as there is no reason to chase them if you are three or four days too late. As they say in San Francisco, "Another cable car comes along about every 15 minutes."

(15) *Take action when the accumulation/distribution index indicates a shift in supply and demand.* This is the signal you are waiting for and it can tell you more than the chart pattern of the stock by itself.

(16) *Never wait out another MBI cycle while remaining in an unsuccessful option position.* If you were wrong in your prediction for the current cycle, there is no valid reason to think the next cycle will bail you out. The time value portion of the option premium will continue to

deteriorate rapidly before the next market cycle peak occurs and the total option value will be much less, even though the stock price may have stayed the same. If the stock fails to trend higher and turns down during the next cycle, you can be wiped out.

(17)   *Be ready to sell all long call positions when the MBI indicator makes a top,* which usually takes two or three days to form. Distribution is usually present in your stock's accumulation/distribution line at the same time, and the options can be sold while the stock is still in the upward trend channel before other traders spot the reversal.

(18)   *Place limit orders on buy positions.* This does not mean you should not be in at the asked price or above, but at least limit the price you will pay. In some cases, while you should be sure of getting your order filled, you still need to ask yourself how much you are willing to pay for the option. Do not let your enthusiasm rule your reason.

(19)   *If your option position goes up 100 percent, but you expect it to go still further, sell at least fifty percent of your position, and let the rest ride.* This allows you to recover your original investment and still have further potential. You also free some capital for another position. This is a good tactic when the accumulation/distribution line remains extremely strong, and the stock is in a steep uptrend, or when you suspect a measured move. On the average these moves happen only two or three times a year.

(20)   *Watch the stock closely if some good news is released on a stock while you are in a long position.* If it goes up or churns on high volume, it is better to sell at that time.

(21)   *Call options are best sold on strong market days* and should generally be placed at the market or bid price when you decide to sell. *Put options are best sold on weak market days* and should generally be placed at the market or bid price when you decide to sell.

(22)   *If you do not have a profit in five days, close the position at the market.* You were wrong in your initial judgment, and the sooner you admit it, the better off your account balance will be. Always remember you are working with a short-term system and long-term movements are completely out of the realm of your measurements. Do not be trapped into a long-term position based on short-term parameters.

(23)   *Close a position after a 30 percent loss, or if the stock has not moved in the first five trading days.* Remain flexible, cut your losses, and wait for a better opportunity. You can predict targets, but never argue when events prove you wrong.

(24) *Never argue with a trend-channel break; it costs too much money.* After you are in a position, a trend-channel should develop for the stock as it trades higher. Establish the boundaries of the channel and sketch it in with two parallel lines. If the stock breaks its upward trend-line, sell at the market.

(25) *Never feel so certain of any one situation that you put 100 percent of your money and confidence into it.* Diversification is important for hedging risks. Twenty percent of your option capital is the most that should be put into any one position at one time. Five positions are about all you can follow properly at one time.

(26) *Keep your plotting work up to date.* A hit-or-miss approach will cause you to make wrong decisions. Your work will become distorted, you will lose your place and your feel for the market. You will not be ready for the really good reversals if you approach the market in a haphazard manner. With up-to-date data that you compile yourself you will be three to seven days ahead of any chart service or stock market advisory material that can be mailed to you.

(27) *Try your best to trade the trends mechanically and unemotionally.* This is the hardest task you will ever face in trading options or any other speculative trading. You must master your emotions, or you will lose money.

(28) *Try to separate yourself from concern for money.* Look only at the movement of the stocks as they trade and take action on these movements. The dollars will take care of themselves, if you are right more often than wrong.

(29) *Do your own thinking.* Be willing to listen to others and continue learning, but only take action when all the technical conditions line up properly.

(30) *Be honest with yourself and do not blame others or the market for your failures.* The responsibility for your trading results is yours, and yours alone.

SIXTEEN

Analysis of Charted Stocks

In this chapter we are going to see the results of charting nine major option stocks for a one year period, September 1978 through August 1979. In order to help you understand how my method works, I have combined on each chart three main elements—the stock price action line (bar chart), the accumulation/distribution line on the stock, and at the bottom, the overall market indicator, the MBI. (In real practice you would not keep the MBI on every chart—you would use a separate one you could use to lay over a stock chart to make comparisons.)

We will consider each element separately, and then combine them. I repeat some material presented earlier in the book because it is necessary at this point to summarize what we are doing as we go along.

Envelope bands have been drawn to enclose the stock price action. Not included are the mid-band on the envelope, trendlines, trend-channels, and all the other notations that *could* be made in analyzing a stock chart, because so many lines crossing and recrossing each other would be confusing. It is also a good learning technique for you to analyze the trades yourself for practice as you study the charts. You may want to take a colored pencil and add these lines, now that you know how to draw them.

If you don't want to mark up your book, run some Xerox copies of the charts—several of each—and experiment with them. Cut apart a copy of the Dow chart and overlay it on the others for a comparison of reversal points, cycles, strength or weakness comparisons, and so on.

135

Cut off the MBI and move it up close to the price line or the accumulation/distribution line for closer comparison. The dates on all the charts match up, so you can shift them around and learn a lot from this.

Mark up the copies with trendlines, signals, mid-bands—whatever you like. Try to pick out cycles. Compare cycles in a stock with cycles in the Dow. As a learning process this can't be beat! (You can also get a published chartbook and do more of the same. Trial subscriptions are available at little cost, or perhaps your broker can obtain an old chartbook for you to practice with.)

The two symbols I have used on the charts, the numbered circles and the arrows, are used to point out to you some good trades that could have been selected by using my method. The arrows point to trendline breaks that occurred as a reversal was formed. They coincide with similar reversals in the accumulation/distribution line and the MBI. The odd-numbered circles are buy signals and the even-numbered circles are sell signals. I have not attempted to highlight *every* buy and sell signal—just the ones my method was likely to pick up.

(No attempt was made to highlight possible put trades. During the period covered by the charts, only a few stocks had puts available. On May 6, 1980, the Securities and Exchange Commission authorized exchanges to list 63 additional put options, and cleared the way for trading to begin in many more stocks. By the time this book is published, the list of stocks having calls and puts available will have been greatly expanded.)

I have shown some trades that were not spectacularly successful, and even presented a few that in all likelihood did not provide much profit. I have presented a variety of charts—ones that turned out to be good trading stocks, one or two that were disappointing, and a couple of stocks that split during the period. The reality of everyday trading won't give you winners every time. Anyone using hindsight could have picked out a group of super stocks with terrific moves, charted them, and used them to back up his system. (Indeed, I have long suspected that this is *exactly* what authors of some of the technical books I have read actually did.) It is my intention to give you an accurate impression of what to expect, based on my *own daily charting* as it evolved day by day during the period of September 1978 through August 1979. The good and the bad alike are displayed here. They are representative of what might be expected to happen in real life.

Of the nine charted stocks presented here, three are components of the Dow Jones Industrial Average—Du Pont, Minnesota Mining & Manufacturing, and Merck. If you follow a few of the large Dow stocks, you will find that some of them track quite well with the DJIA cycles. You will have the added plus of confirmation when the Dow is turning up or down, and seeing it happen in the Dow stocks you track. If you compare these three stocks with the Dow chart for the same period, you will find that Du Pont tracked *perfectly* with the Dow, and offered some spectacular trades. MMM, on the other had, was in a long-term downtrend most of the year. Although it tracked well with the Dow, the opportunities for profitable trades were few. Merck, for the most part, *did not* always track with the Dow, and at times it was much stronger than the Dow.

But now, let us consider each of the three elements separately to see how we can get the most out of them, and then put them *together* with most interesting results.

THE PRICE ACTION LINE

As price action develops on your chart (Figure 20) draw in a *trendline* (A). In an uptrend, *bottoms* are connected. A second line can then be drawn parallel to the trendline (B) to establish a *trend-channel*. (Dashes are used here to differentiate between the trendline and trend-channel boundary.) Buy calls on the breakout. A *trendline break* occurs when price action breaks out of the channel, indicating it is time to sell (or close out) your *call* position (C).

In a downtrend, *tops* are connected to establish the trendline (D). Buy puts when downtrend begins. Establish the trend-channel boundary along bottoms in downtrend (E). A break of the trendline on the upside says *sell* (or close out) your *put* position (F). It is possible that a call position can be taken immediately if all other factors say go (G).

Remember, price action does not *always* follow a very tight channel; be flexible—move your lines to accommodate some irregular movement, and don't be too arbitrary if you sense a wider or a curved channel is developing. Don't hesitate to cut off a few little tips that do not fit (see Figure 21). What we are striving for is a sense of the boundaries of the channel—just like the envelope boundaries, they are subject to change,

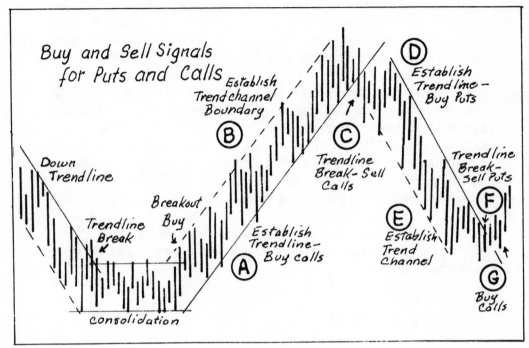

Figure 20. Using trendlines for signals.

and may need to be adjusted several times as price action develops. When in doubt, watch what the accumulation/distribution line is doing. If you see a break, watch carefully.

THE STEWART ACCUMULATION/DISTRIBUTION LINE

As you plot the Stewart accumulation/distribution line beneath the stock price action, notice if the two are moving approximately together. Watch for similar patterns in both lines—a triangle, flag, consolidation or reversal in one usually appears in the other. The accumulation/distribution line tends to confirm what you see happening in the stock price action.

When increased volume appears, the accumulation/distribution will sometimes give you a strong signal before it is reflected in the price action. This is one of the things to watch for.

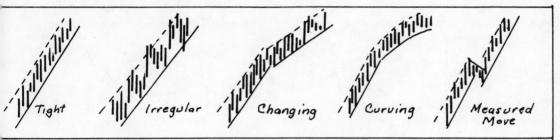

Figure 21. Some types of trendlines.

A falling off of volume is also a signal. This appears as a flattening out or sideways movement in the accumulation/distribution line. This can mean a consolidation, or an impending change of direction. A breakout from this flattened line tells you which way the stock is likely to go.

Reversals often occur ahead of price action; this divergence can be a strong action signal, and one you had better not ignore. (Go back to Chapter 10 and study Figures 16, 17, and 18 again.)

Trendlines can be drawn on the accumulation/distribution line, just as you do on price action line (see Figure 17 and 18). Frequently you can detect longer-term accumulation not yet evident in stock price this way.

All of these things could be called forms of divergence. When divergence is present in any form something is likely to happen sooner or later to bring the two elements back in balance.

The Stewart accumulation/distribution line gives you a way to measure what volume is doing to the stock's price, and acts as confirmation to your decisions based on stock price trendline breaks and suspected reversals, and MBI action points. Frequently it will warn you to be careful, or that your decision is incorrect. Used along with price action and the MBI, the accumulation/distribution line becomes a very useful tool for short-term option trading.

HOW TO HANDLE SCALE AND SPLITS

If you find the accumulation/distribution line does not show much movement and is hard to analyze, perhaps a change of scale will make features more apparent:

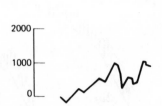

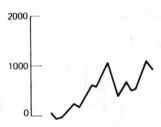

Similarly, an accumulation/distribution line that continually runs all over the paper is hard to interpret. If you find this happening, it can be tamed by plotting it on a smaller scale:

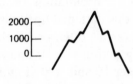

If stocks are plotted using several different scales you are likely to become confused and make mistakes as you go from one chart to the next. If possible, keep them all to the same scale unless you really must change them. Generally, a stock that has a small capitalization, a low Beta, or a small and consistent daily volume will have a relatively compact accumulation/distribution line. A stock with a large capitalization, a high Beta, or high average daily volume is the kind that will have an accumulation/distribution line that runs off the paper. If you do not want to change the scale, another technique is simply to break the accumulation/distribution line at the point where a massive volume day occurs, mark the scale number by the break, and start the line again lower on the page, again putting in the scale number where the break occurred. (For examples see Hewlett Packard, Figure 28 and Xerox, Figure 32.)

Broad, long-term trendlines can sometimes be established for the accumulation/distribution line, just as they can for the stock price line. These should agree with the general long-term trend of the stock.

Stock splits occur frequently enough that you are bound to have a few of them crop up on your charts during a given year. Ideally, when a split occurs a chart should be completely redrawn and all the calculations and plotted data adjusted to reflect the split. However, a busy person with a career just will not have time for this. Common sense says just break the lines and start over with the split prices and new accumulation/distribution figures. Since chart services always adjust their charts immediately, you can refer to one for the overall pattern.

THE MOVING BALANCE INDICATOR

The MBI's major use is in timing market turns. It is primarily designed to be an overbought/oversold indicator, and should always be coordinated with the other two elements to ensure proper timing.

Also keep in mind that the envelope boundaries in a stock and in the Dow represent *overbought* and *oversold* just as these conditions are measured in the MBI. They usually move in tandem; the stock (or the Dow) hits its short-term oversold line (the top edge-band) about the same time that the MBI reverses and turns down. On MBI bottoms, the opposite occurs; the stock reverses at the lower envelope band, representing oversold (see Figure 22).

If more review is needed on the MBI, refer to Chapter 9.

Now we are ready to put the three elements together. We watch the MBI for a *bottom reversal* (confirmed by the 5 day moving average), compare the MBI status with the position of the Dow in its trading envelope, look for *accumulation beginning in the Dow* (has it been oversold too?), and look for *signs of a trendline break to the upside in the Dow.* We watch our charted stocks (or ones in a chart service) for *trend-channel breaks to the upside,* for *breakouts from consolidation patterns,* and for *unusual volume.* We watch the accumulation/distribution line for each stock for *reversals, breakouts on unusual volume,* and *strong divergence.*

When the three elements are in phase, the situation tells you that a good trade is likely. *Important note:* sometimes strong (or very weak) stocks defy MBI cycles. In these cases, strong unbroken trend-channels and strong unbroken accumulation allow you to take positions or stay in established ones longer than the MBI would suggest. Remember the MBI reflects the *overall* market. An individual stock often goes against the

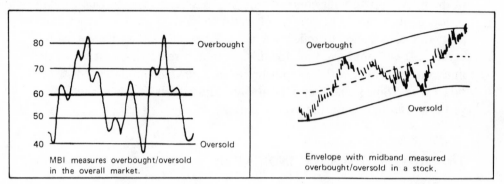

Figure 22. The MBI and stock *usually* reverse in tandem.

tide. See Atlantic Richfield, Figure 24, and Hewlett-Packard, Figure 28. When this is occurring let the trend-channel break or break in accumulation be your guide to get out. Be sure to keep in mind the special cases (see the Special Note in Chapter 11) where very strong moves in the Dow and the Dow Accumulation/Distribution Index override the short-term oscillations in the MBI. There will be times, such as the very strong bull market in the Spring of 1980, when the MBI will just oscillate in a narrow range in overbought territory and not give a valid short-term signal until the Dow and the Dow Accumulation/Distribution Index does.

Generally, MBI bottoms are sharper and better defined for trend reversals than tops. You usually have four to five days in which to sell at an MBI top before the market starts trending downward.

Sometimes trendlines can be drawn connecting MBI tops. If a top is significantly lower than the one preceding it, connect them in a down-trending line. Bottoms similarly can be connected. Intermediate-term strength or weakness in the market sometimes can be deduced from this, and major trend changes can develop in this way, climaxing in an *unusually high* MBI top or an *unusually low* bottom. These are usually *major reversals* (see Dow Chart, MBI points 5 and 8, Figure 23).

When the market does not move with a strong uptrending MBI move, it is weak. The DJIA should move up in tandem with the MBI. If it diverges, that is, if there is little change in the Dow average as the MBI goes up, you have a weak or sideways movement with no power (point 15, Figure 23).

If you do not get a strong definable uptrend in the DJIA after ten days

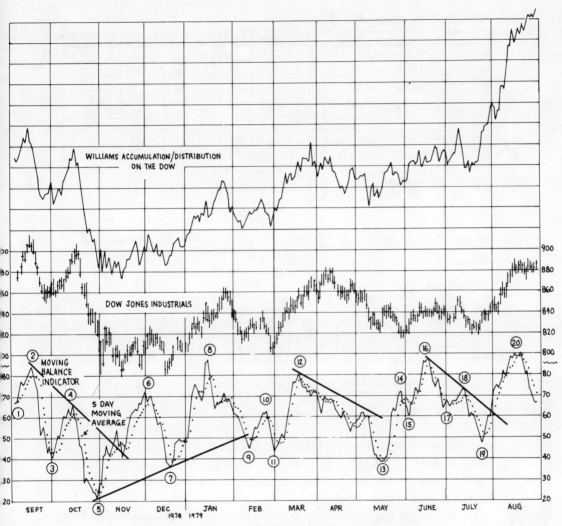

Figure 23. Dow Jones/MBI chart with trendlines on MBI.

143

Date <u>Tuesday, August 28, 1979</u>

Stock	High	Low	Close	Net Chg.	Volume	Acc/Dis*
ARC Atlantic Richfield	70.4	70.0	70.1	- .1	536	- 134
GLW Corning Glass Works	64.6	64.0	64.2	--	105	--
DEC Digital Equipment	64.0	63.1	63.5	- .1	1042	- 116
DD Du Pont	43.1	42.6	43.0	+ .1	450	+ 90
HWP Hewlett Packard	56.2	55.5	55.9	+ .4	419	+ 239
MRK Merck	70.2	69.8	70.0	+ .2	438	+ 219
MMM Minnesota Mining & Mfg.	55.1	54.8	54.9	--	1524	--
SLB Schlumberger	86.4	85.5	86.0	--	731	--
XRX Xerox	67.8	66.9	67.2	- .4	823	- 366

$*Acc/Dis = \dfrac{Net\ Chg.}{H - L} \times Vol. = \pm$ (Stewart Method)

MBI TABLE

Volume of Advancing Stocks 12,850

Volume of Declining Stocks 11,230

(1) Advances 671

(2) Declines 744

$$\dfrac{Adv.}{Decl.} \div \dfrac{Adv.Vol.}{Decl.Vol.} = MKDS\ Index$$

$$\dfrac{671}{744} \div \dfrac{12,850}{11,230} = .788$$

	Open	High	Low	Close	Volume	Acc/Dis **
Dow Jones Index	885.41	889.68	881.40	884.64	2,363	- 219.7

**Williams Method for the Dow Industrials:

$$Acc\ /Dis = \dfrac{Close - Open}{High - Low} \times Volume = \pm$$

$$\dfrac{884.64 - 885.41}{889.68 - 881.40} \times 2,363 = -219.7$$

of a sharply uptrending MBI, there is no great upside potential in that swing (points 13–14, 15–16. It must be pointed out, however, that during this same period, good gains are seen in many individual stocks. The Dow is not the whole story.

Do not forget the Master Checklist in Chapter 13, and remember that it is a good idea to fill out the Option Trading Checklist form too, when considering an option trade. This will catch some of the factors you may have missed and will give you a record of your transaction for future study.

Don't forget that we are trying to predict 10–15 percent moves in stock prices as they move from oversold to overbought, and we want to *time* the trades with the best precision we can. That is the basis for the reliability and profitability of this system and we must constantly be alert for the proper factors to be in place *before* we take a position.

Opposite is a daily worksheet form that I use to record the plotting data for the stocks shown in this chapter. It is easy to use and has places for gathering the MBI data and the Dow figures, which are kept up to date daily.

STUDYING THE CHARTS IN THIS CHAPTER

The final nine charts in this book (Figures 24–32) should be studied in the following manner to learn how the three elements work together:

1. Place the edge of a piece of paper vertically in line with one of the numbered buy points (odd numbers are buy points, even numbers indicate trendline breaks, signaling a sell).
2. Notice the MBI. Has a bottom formed? Does it appear to be turning up? Does the 5 day moving average confirm this? (The 5 day moving average on the MBI is the dotted line on the Dow Jones chart, Figure 23, and the Corning chart, Figure 25.)
3. Look at the Stewart accumulation/distribution line. No more selling pressure evident? Has strong accumulation begun or has a reversal or a consolidation pattern with a breakout of accumulation formed?
4. Look at the price action line. Has it hit the lower edge-band? Is it in a consolidation pattern? Does it look like it is reversing? Has the downtrend line broken? Is it making a rounding bottom?

    If you can answer yes for at least one of these questions for each element, they are probably in phase and a buy may be indicated.
5. Slide the paper to the right a little bit. Were you right? If yes,
6. The MBI will go up.
7. Accumulation will come in.
8. Stock will rise in price.
9. Slide the paper over. The MBI top will be forming. Accumulation may be stalled, forming a reversal, or failing. Stock may be breaking trendline, hitting envelope band, or stalling. Sell.

As you repeat this process with each marked move on each of the charts presented, try to imagine how each trade would actually develop in day-to-day trading. See if you were right and how much stock movement you could have captured. Keep the future action covered with a piece of paper, sliding it to the right to check developments as they actually occur and compare the results with what you expected to happen.

You will begin to see that the three elements do not always move in phase. You will miss some good moves because of this. You will buy sometimes on expectations that do not develop. And, you will surprise yourself sometimes and get extremely strong moves in which accumulation and price action defy the MBI. When this happens, stay in the position until the trendline breaks, and sell on the break. When a trade does not progress and develop within five days, get out. Note how many times this turns out to be the correct action. If a trade begins to turn against you, always cut your losses by selling the option.

By practicing in the above manner, you can learn a lot about trading options. You can employ the same technique with a published chartbook, of course, without the accumulation/distribution line for an individual stock. If you have the MBI plotted for the period, you can compare cycles and reversals of the stock with the overall movement of this indicator.

You will notice on some of these charts that a long-term trendline in the accumulation/distribution line can be established. A stock that has a continuous trend of net accumulation is a good stock for trading call options, especially if its relative strength is greater than the market average.

A stock with a falling long-term accumulation/distribution line is avoided for trading calls, but might prove a good one for puts if they are available. Minnesota Mining & Manufacturing is an example of a stock with a downtrending accumulation/distribution, but it had no put options (see Figure 30). It provides little of interest to us, and probably should be ignored for call trading until the long-term trend turns up.

ANALYSIS OF NINE SELECTED STOCKS
CHARTED BY THE AUTHOR
DURING THE ONE YEAR PERIOD,
SEPTEMBER, 1978–AUGUST, 1979

Atlantic Richfield was selected as a stock to chart because it was in the strong oil group and showed great relative strength. Even though the average price was around $60 per share, the envelope width was only 4½ points and the stock stayed in a continuous tight uptrend. This stock was so strong that it defied the overall market indicator, the MBI, most of the time and was only in phase with it at points 1, 3, 5, and 7.

The accumulation/distribution line gave you more trading signals, but because some of them were out of phase with the MBI, I would have left most of them alone.

Points 1, 3, 5, and 7 provided safe buy signals; points 2, 4, 6, and 8 provided sell signals. Because of the relatively narrow envelope, trading possibilities were limited to small moves.

A stock that is trading in a strong uptrend like this one provides swings of about 5–6 percent. After a major cyclic top has formed, the envelope should widen and sharper corrections should occur, making the stock more attractive for option trading.

(Puts became available for trading in this stock in May 1980.)

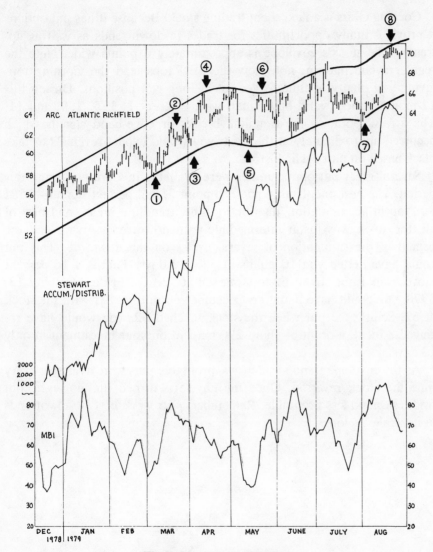

Figure 24. Atlantic Richfield.

149

Corning Glass is an excellent trading stock. Because it has put options it provides many opportunities for trades in downtrends as well as uptrends. The stock's envelope is approximately 6 points wide. Note the regular cyclic pattern; note how the MBI tops lead the Corning tops giving you plenty of time to get out of long call positions. During this 12-month period, valid buy signals were given at 1, 3, 5, 7, 9, and 11. The arrows point to the trendline breaks or edge-band signals which occurred approximately at the times you would expect reversals to take place based on past cyclic history.

Several great put opportunities were avaliable in Corning during this period. The best one, from point 2 to point 3, had perfect signals—MBI top, top in accumulation/distribution line, trendline break, and best of all, the stock was in an intermediate-term downtrend, giving you the benefit of the summation of several cycles on the downside. This put could have netted you 10 points in only 12 days. That is a 16 percent move from a put buy at 62 to a put sell at 52.) On Friday, October 13, 1978, you could have bought a December 60 put for 2¾ with the stock at 62. Selling the put when the stock reached 52, you would have received 8 for it, a profit of about 290 percent on your investment in only 12 days.

As the envelope trended sideways, profitable puts were available every time the stock reversed. Once the envelope turned up, however, put trades became less profitable. Remember, *puts* work best in downtrends or neutral envelopes.

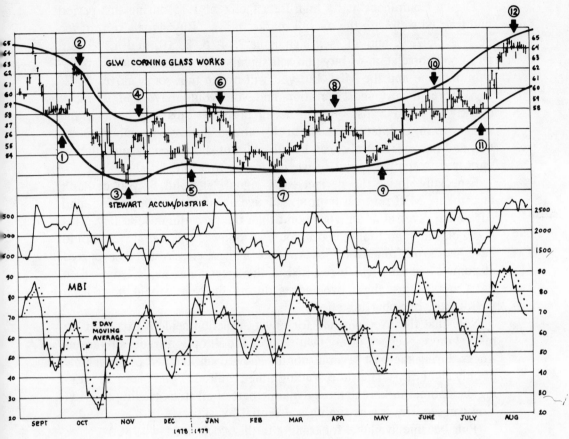

Figure 25. Corning Glass.

Digital Equipment had a high-Beta factor of 1.75 during this period and tracked well with the overall market moves. Buy signals were given at 1, 3, 5, 7, 9, and 11; sell signals at 2, 4, 6, 8, 10, and 12. There was good correlation of buy and sell signals with the accumulation/distribution line and the MBI, but you will notice that some moves (1–2, 3–4) were of very short duration and you would have had to move quickly to avoid a loss once in a call position. This was because the stock was in an intermediate-term downtrend during September, October, and part of December, and really did not show much accumulation until mid-December (point 5) when it really took off.

Especially notice the perfect entry signals at point 5 (you couldn't miss them), MBI reversal bottom, massive accumulation beginning, and edge-band reversal at a higher point than the preceding cyclic low. This was a classic opportunity, and if you had followed this signal, you would have had a run from 48 to 58. Another of these classic signals occurred at point 11 in July which resulted in the spectacular move from 54 to 64! Catching just these two moves during the year would have been well worth your charting effort.

Note that the average time for any transaction seldom exceeded 15 market days. A check of my own records for all option trades in various stocks during the past several months showed an average position time of only eight days. The short trading time required is one factor in making the option market the most dynamic part of all stock trading activity. You can see why expert timing is essential for success.

(Puts became available for trading in this stock in May 1980.)

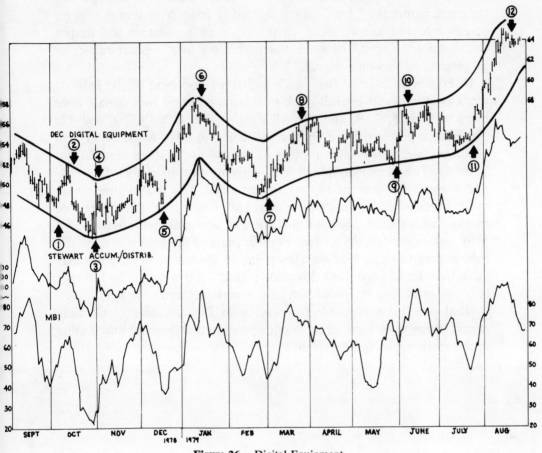

Figure 26. Digital Equipment.

153

DuPont was trading in the $125–140 range during the first part of the chart, before the 3 for 1 split at the end of June. Note that the range, or envelope width, was about 13 points or 10 percent on the unsplit stock. After the split, the stock started trading in a 4 point range, or 10 percent, as we would expect.

DuPont is an average-Beta stock and is a component of the Dow so it tracks closely with overall stock market movements. Buy signals were given at 1, 3, 5, 7, 9, and 11; sell signals at 2, 4, 6, 8, 10, and 12. The author purchased ten October 40 calls for $2\frac{1}{16}$ at point 11 and sold them twelve days later at point 12 for $4\frac{1}{2}$ as the stock moved from 39 to 43. This is an example of a 10 percent move in a stock that produced over a 100 percent appreciation in a call. This is also an example of the purchase of an out-of-the-money call, near the striking price, coinciding with a strong upward movement of accumulation after a sharp MBI bottom formed. As advised in other parts of the text, it is normally safer to purchase calls that are a few points in-the-money or have intrinsic value in order to have some downside protection if wrong. The leverage is not as great, but the profit potential is certainly safer.

(Had puts been available for trading in DuPont during this time period, there were some great profit opportunities present. Put trading in this stock began in May 1980.)

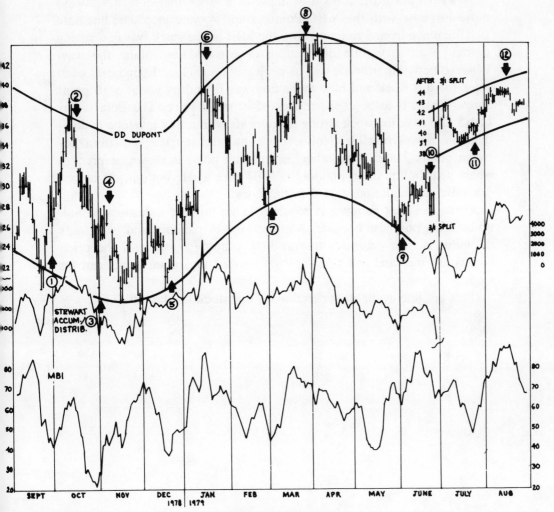

Figure 27. DuPont.

155

Hewlett Packard is a good example of a stock that does not always move in phase with the MBI. Points 3 and 4 were in phase, but note that the move from 5 to 6 overtook the MBI as the stock was in a strong uptrend with very little distribution or consolidation along the way. Observe how important it was to project the envelope boundaries each week for this stock and how the action was bound by about a 10 point spread which is to be expected for a $90 stock price. The Beta factor of 1.5 also gave the stock strong movements within this envelope making dynamic moves possible. Notice the continuation triangle pattern between points 7 and 8. Another perfect buy point is shown at point 9 where distribution dried up and the MBI gave a safe bottom just before dramatic accumulation started in the stock.

Remember that patience is required in waiting for indicators to line up before a purchase is made. Another kind of patience and good self-discipline is then necessary to stay in a winning move until the price targets are met and sell signals given so that maximum profit can be made.

(Puts became available for trading in this stock in May 1980.)

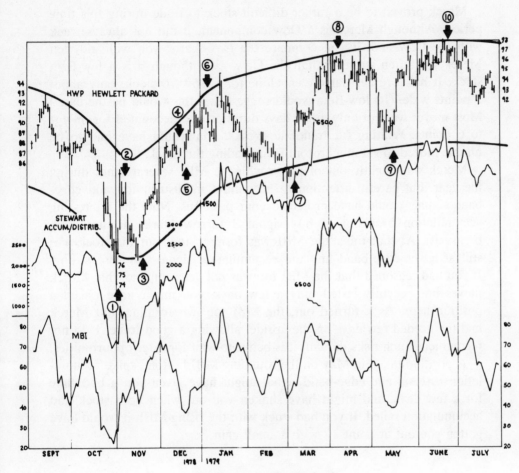

Figure 28. Hewlett Packard.

Merck proved to be a rather difficult stock to trade during this time period. Although Merck is a Dow component, it did not always track with the Dow and, if you compare the two charts, you will find that Merck was often stronger than the Dow, even though it is a low-Beta stock. It has a rather narrow envelope for a $60–70 stock, only about 5 points wide. (Its low-Beta would suggest that this would be the case.) Most moves were of only a few days duration and accounted for only 4 to 6 points. Waiting for trendline breaks, you would have had to be nimble indeed to get much profit from trading this stock.

Merck was slightly out of phase with the MBI several times during the year, but careful attention to accumulation/distribution and edge-band signals would have protected your positions. Note the interesting accumulation breakout at buy signal 3 (arrow marks accumulation breakout). At that time, the MBI was forming top, but the stock was still at lower edge-band and the accumulation signal was very strong. If you had reasoned that the MBI top was not yet complete, that Merck moves had recently lasted only a few days, you might have risked a position here. As it turned out, the MBI top *was* forming, but Merck had the needed few days on the upside, allowing a good trade. I do not recommend such risks though; it is better to wait for safer opportunities.

A position taken in May on the rounding MBI bottom, spike accumulation reversal and edge-band signal might have given you a bad time for a few days, and might have shaken you out when both stock and accumulation failed. If you had stuck with the rising MBI, it would have gotten you out at point 12 with a small gain.

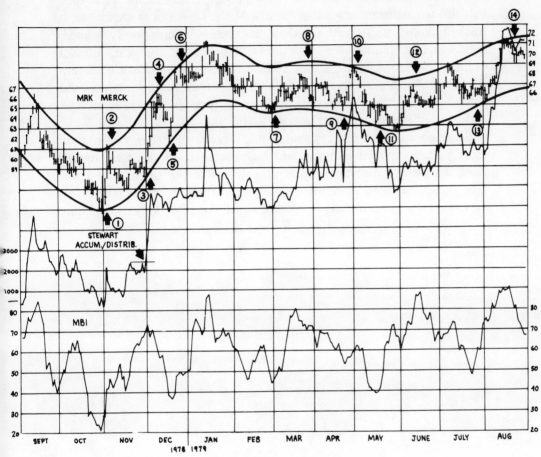

Figure 29. Merck.

159

Minnesota Mining, another Dow component, is an example of a stock that did not perform as well as the rest of the Dow stocks. Although it tracked almost exactly with the Dow, the up moves were poorly defined. Stocks in downtrends, like this one was for most of the year, are not exciting to follow although they can be traded profitably on occasion, when valid signals are given. Its 6 point wide envelope suggests it would provide more action than it did. Buy signals were given at 1, 3, 5, 7, 9, and 11; sell signals were at 2, 4, 6, 8, 10, and 12.

Remember at the MBI reversal points there are other more dynamic chart patterns available that could be selected from the total option stock list on a comparative basis. Regardless of the stocks you track with the Accumulation/Distribution Index, it always pays to scan all the option stocks for trading possibilities at the time MBI reversals occur.

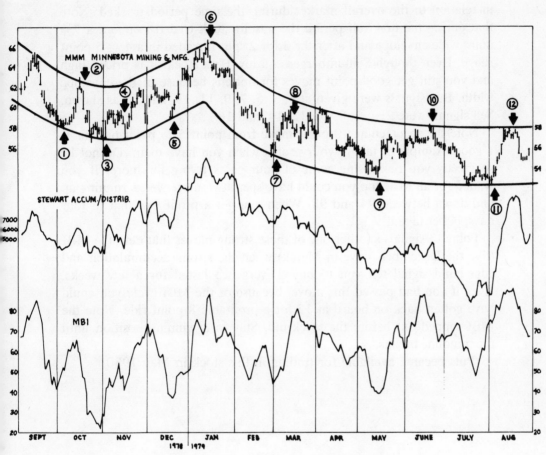

Figure 30. Minnesota Mining & Manufacturing.

Schlumberger was among those stocks that had a high relative strength in relation to the overall market during the time period tracked. Note that during the first half period the unsplit stock traded in about a 7½ point wide envelope and after the 3 for 2 split it traded in a 4½–5 point range. Even though Schlumberger is a low-Beta stock, it is priced high and you still get good point moves for options because of the envelope width. Buy signals were given at 1, 3, 5, 7, 9, 11, 13, and 15 as shown. Sell signals were 2, 4, 6, 8, 10, 12, 14, and 16.

Note the spectacular 10 point move from point 5 to point 6. This is a good example of taking your profits when you have them. Do not be so greedy you risk losing some of your gains trying for more. If you waited for an MBI top you could have spent two more weeks running up and down between 94 and 98. When you get a profit like that in four days, better take it!

Point 13 signals another one of those strong moves that defy the MBI (like the December move in Merck) when the strong accumulation and edge-band signal tell you to buy. Divergence lasted for a few weeks. Even if you had passed this move, because of the MBI cycle you could have gotten back on board at 15 for a profitable 8 point ride. Note the MBI topped out before the stock did. Stay in a winning position until the trendline breaks.

(Puts became available for trading in this stock in May 1980.)

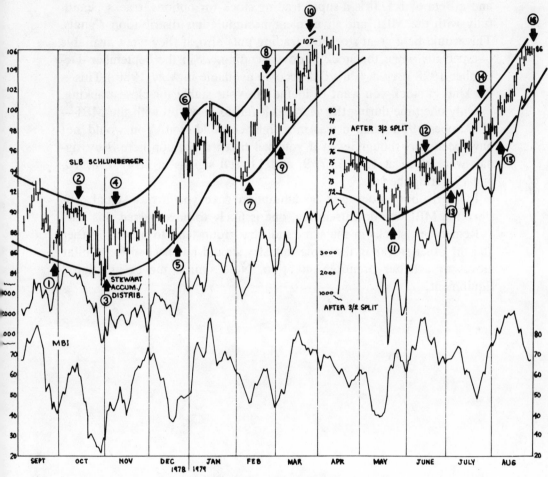

Figure 31. Schlumberger.

Xerox has an envelope width of about 6 points, good periodic swings, and a Beta of 1.5. It is a super trading stock for options, tracks beautifully with the MBI, and gives clear accumulation/distribution signals. This would be a great stock for trading puts also, if they were available —especially when the stock is downtrending, as in the September–December 1978 period. (Puts did become available in May 1980.) This is the kind of stock you want to include in your stable for close tracking.

Only one time during the year did it fail to move up with the MBI— in October 1978 when it was in a tight consolidation. You would not have been hurt though, even if you had taken a position here. Buy signals were given at 1, 3, 5, 7, 9, and 11; sell signals at 2, 4, 6, 8, 10, and 12 during the year.

In April, both stock and accumulation gave you a buy signal, but since the MBI was downtrending, one is likely to have passed this one.

Remember, stocks in the same industry group tend to move together and the other stocks in the same industry should be checked for similar moves or a better premium situation. Note similar moves in Digital Equipment.

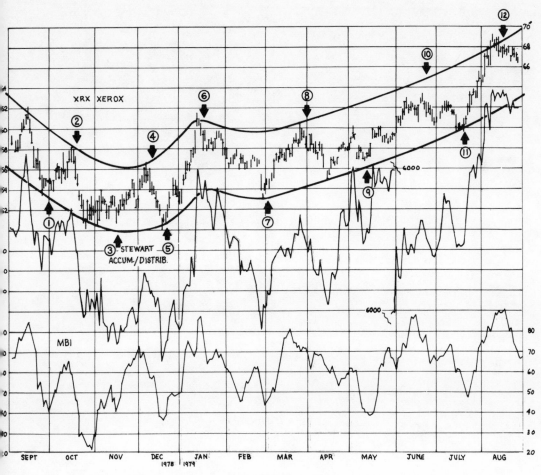

Figure 32. Xerox.

165

SEVENTEEN

Profile of a Professional Trader

We should be thankful that we live in a country that allows us the freedom of choice to move our capital around where it will earn the greatest return. There is no place in the world where there is a greater opportunity to accomplish this than Wall Street.

When you actively trade in stocks and stock options, you are up against the best financial minds. They are going to take money away from those who are less skilled and knowledgeable about the market. These are the professionals who operate in the market on a full-time basis. They are the true capitalists. They know how to use their capital in the most advantageous ways, and are quick to move it around for the most mileage. These traders make their whole livelihood from the market. Every day they face the acid test of fully relying on their own skills and experience. They know how to use their assets to make them grow. The ones who are proven successful over the long term are held in awe by money managers, stock brokers, traders, and others who admire their skills and are envious of their abilities.

A novice or a casual participant is not going to beat the professional. We would not think of attempting surgery, or practicing law or engineering without the years of special training required for these professions. Just think of all the highly specialized professions for which we are unsuited and untrained. No one would be so foolhardy as to jump into these areas and try to muddle through the requirements or "fly by the seat of his pants." Yet that is exactly what the majority of individual speculators do—acting on tips, brokers touts, rumors, and so forth, they buy enthusiastically just as rallies fade. This group then panics and sells when it sees stocks "fall out of bed." You will not find our professional doing these things because he works full time and his complete effort is dedicated to being successful at his chosen occupation.

We want to learn as much as we can about how these full-time traders operate so that we can have a reasonable degree of success on a part-time basis. I do not know any of these "pure" traders personally, but I will outline some of the characteristics I think they must have and use in order to stay consistently ahead of the crowd, which includes the public, institutional fund managers, as well as most of the rest of us.

First, a successful trader must be psychologically prepared to expect a reasonable opportunity for making money in the market. This means he must weigh the odds and then make a prediction on future stock price movement for profit potential. He must also have the staying power to stick with the trend once he is in a position in order to let profit build. In other words, a smart trader does not take very small profits, but gives his correct decisions time to work out in the marketplace. Often a novice finds it very difficult emotionally to stay in a profitable position and quickly takes only a small part of the potential gains. It does you no good to be right about the buy decision if you sell too soon.

A trader has become successful by working at it over a period of years. He does not arrive at a competent level without study, experience, and evaluation. He appreciates the fact that it is difficult to trade in the market, he respects the abilities of the others he is trading against, and he guards against overconfidence after making a series of correct trades. He backs off occasionally to get a new perspective, because he knows that the market has a way of leveling overconfidence quickly.

The trader is a very independent person and has developed his own style. He does not operate by consulting several other people before arriving at his own decisions. He has a drive to make money because he feels that money means freedom in this society, and that it ensures the independence he wants.

After weighing the facts in a situation and making a decision, he acts quickly because his thinking is clear and his decision definite. He never forgets that, as in any other enterprise, he must buy at wholesale and sell at retail to make a profit and stay in business. Because of this he does not chase stocks, and he seldom buys at the highest price for the day. He tries to place his orders to buy on down or slow days and at the low for the day. He picks his buy points after a consolidation or a reversal in prices has occurred. He waits for signals before he takes a position.

Since he knows that correct timing is the most important factor, he keeps up to date with overall market movements so that he can pinpoint changes in trends. Once a trend is established he trades with the trend until it reverses. He never argues with a trendline break.

The successful trader lets stocks tell him what to do and not vice versa. He weighs what people or publications say about stocks, but he acts only on evidence that stocks are actually being accumulated or distributed. Their trading action in the market tells the story.

The professional does not take unnecessary risks in the market by trading options that are out-of-the-money. He is always concerned about how much he can lose when he is wrong, and cuts his losses at the first indication that things are not right. He is not looking for the occasional big long shot with accompanying high risks, but he will participate if other factors are right. He feels more comfortable trading stocks within boundaries that he can predict and measure consistently. He concentrates on reasonable, steady returns.

The active trader does not spend all his time waiting for big moves or trying to predict large market changes, but trades within the existing framework that the market has already traced out. He will still be in at the right time, whether it is just for a ripple or the start of a large wave movement. Since he is active and up to date, he will not get trapped for very long when the market makes major reversals. He gets out of the way quickly. He is honest and admits it when he is wrong, and sells at the market to preserve most of his capital.

I think the single most important trait the successful trader has is control over his emotions. To the greatest extent possible, he separates his emotions from his money and thinks of stocks only as lines and trends on a piece of chart paper. This allows him to be objective about his judgments and actions.

To summarize, the professional trader must:

- Be highly motivated, ambitious, curious, competitive, independent, open-minded, flexible, decisive.
- Do the necessary homework, keep up to date on the market and trends in the economy, then trade in the existing framework, whether long or short.

- Let profits accrue and cut losses quickly.
- Avoid foolhardy or unnecessary risks.
- Control his emotions to the best of his ability.
- Continue to study, learn, and improve his techniques.
- Adopt new methods and eliminate those that no longer seem reliable or effective.

What would *your* track record look like today if you had followed the methods used by my ideal professional trader? When you follow his methods and rules you will separate yourself from the crowd. You will buy when the crowd is selling out at wholesale prices, and then you will sell back to them at retail prices. And really, when you get down to the bottom line, that is what trading is all about.

EIGHTEEN

Plan of Action for an Option Trader

In the preceding chapters I outline the methods I use, the rules I follow, and the philosophy that I have developed through experience in option trading. Now it is up to you to determine whether or not you have the personal characteristics necessary for trading options within this framework, and then, if the answer is yes, you can go on to develop your plan of action.

ARE YOU CUT OUT TO BE A SPECULATOR?

First, ask yourself if you have the *motivation* necessary to study, learn, and develop a successful trading technique. Obviously, you must have a deep interest in the market and the drive to work hard at keeping your attention focused on current conditions on a daily basis.

This kind of work requires a lot of *self-discipline*. No matter how good your methods and techniques are, they will not work for you unless you complete the necessary daily work, then follow the trading rules. (This was harder for me, personally, to accomplish than learning to select the correct positions to be in.) Much of the time you will want to jump the gun, shoot from the hip, or "wait just a little bit longer" to see if you are right. If you do these things, you will find that your timing will be wrong, you will pay too much for the option, you will chase the option at a higher price, and you will have missed most of the move.

171

Self-discipline helps you to trade mechanically and takes some of the stress, uncertainty, and emotion out of the decision-making process.

Patience is another virtue one should cultivate. As you follow the market and your stocks, you can expect periods of time that will be uninteresting. You will be bored with charting stocks that are not moving, or a market that seems stalled. You will be tempted to let all your work slide. These periods must be tolerated however, or you will not be prepared for the action signals when they do occur. Often the most powerful moves and the most obvious signals come out of just such dull, uninteresting trading periods. Patience will pay off, believe me!

Are you willing to make a *commitment* of your own hard-earned money? You cannot learn very much from reading a book or attending a lecture. Neither can you accomplish anything by "paper trading." The acid test, and the only test that means anything, is actually committing money to the market—especially if it is money for which you have worked very hard.

You are going to be involved *emotionally* when you make a financial commitment. Can you control your emotions, and make cool decisions based on the facts and the trading rules? Emotion can run high when your own money is at stake; emotions can distort judgment. For instance, suppose you have a good profit in a trade, and the signs tell you it is time to sell. Are you going to let greed keep you in just a little longer? Are you going to let the enthusiasm of others sway you in your decision to take your profit and be satisfied? By the same taken, are you going to let someone talk you out of a winning position when your analysis tells you that you are correct and the trend will continue?

Do you have the *courage* and *ruthlessness* to cut losses short while they are still small, when you realize that you have made a mistake? There is no long-term bailout for incorrect option trades. The results are always losses if you are on the wrong side of the underlying stock movement. Cutting a loss short will leave you with a sense of relief because you have saved some of your capital for the next trade, and because you will feel confident that you can handle either situation—gains or losses—unemotionally.

Up to now, I have not mentioned the *rewards,* other than the obvious one, financial profits. Developing these skills and disciplines will carry over into other aspects of your life and daily business. The self-confidence, the satisfaction, the coolheaded decision-making should sharpen your thinking in other areas of daily endeavor as well.

DEVELOP YOUR PLAN FOR ACTION

You should do about three months of charting and analytic work before attempting to trade options with the methods described in this book. It is necessary to establish enough chart history so that you can develop a sense of timing. You will need to know where you are in terms of the general market and the stocks in which you have particular interest. (Are they in an uptrend, downtrend, neutral, or reversing? Are they strong, weak, overbought, oversold, under accumulation or distribution, and so forth?) You should strive to utilize all the ways to measure and find your place in the market and in your stocks before actually trying to trade. Your charts are your roadmaps. They tell you where you have been and suggest where you are going. Your market indicators help you know what time to leave, how far you are likely to go, how fast your trip is likely to be, and most important, when you have arrived!

Before you actually start trading you need to develop some *confidence* that you can measure and predict the near-term movements. This cannot be done by guessing or by impulse, but only by developing the correct technical skills. Mistakes will be made, but it is virtually impossible to buy into tops and sell at bottoms if you will calculate, plot, and interpret the data each day. If you do this, you will be well ahead of any system or advisory service I have seen for determining short-term moves.

Learn to *set actual goals* and keep these targets in mind at all times. Be *realistic* in your goals; if you cannot see a possible 10–15 percent move in a stock, forget it and go on to the next possibility. You cannot *wish* a stock to move—only supply and demand can make stocks move.

As you prepare yourself to begin trading options, it is necessary to *think through* the present market activity to future possibilities. Most people only think in terms of advances in the market or a stock, but we know that cycles are at work and that they must turn down just as frequently as they turn up. Fine tune your skills so that you are comfortable in any market climate, taking advantage of the downtrends as well as the uptrends. Just be sure that you are trading with the trend. Remember, you do not have to make any heroic predictions about great advances or declines in the averages; you are just trying to capture 10–15 percent moves in stocks. When the larger combined cycle moves *do* occur, you will *still* be in at the correct time and participate in the larger gains available, if you are using the system. I am confident that those of you who apply these methods can move into the elite 5 percent, the highly successful group that makes money.

Writing this book, which covered a time period of one year, has helped my own trading results greatly because it has made me outline the rules and methods that work. I have made and lost considerable amounts of money in the option market in the past. Now I am on the winning side. I have paid the price of admission to the club and do not think anyone can get there by an easy method. I hope you, too, will be able to improve your performance by putting this system into practice.

I might say good luck in your future trading, but you do not need luck; you just need to learn the lessons that bring success and keep trying to improve your skills. My final advice is to stop procrastinating, guessing and dreaming. Start working, measuring and winning!!!

Glossary of Selected Stock and Stock Option Technical Terms

Accumulation.   When there are more buyers than sellers in a stock it is said to be under *accumulation*. Accumulation can be going on in a stock in the early stages of a move without it being apparent in the stock's price. As buying pressure increases, accumulation moves the stock price upward.

Asked price.   Price at which a seller is offering for sale.

Advance/Decline line.   A line plotted on a continuous and cumulative daily basis, showing the net difference between advancing NYSE stocks and declining NYSE stocks.

Advancing volume.   As used in the MBI, the total number of shares that are advancing on the NYSE. This number is found in each day's *Wall Street Journal,* inside the back page, under "Market Diary."

Beta factor.   A term that describes a stock's volatility in terms of how it has moved in relation to the overall market. A Beta of 1.0 would show that the stock has moved exactly with the market average. A Beta of 2.0 indicates the stock is twice as volatile as the market. A Beta of less than 1.0 indicates a stock that has less volatility than the general market. The Beta is usually based on the Standard & Poor's 500 Stock Index.

Buying pressure.   As long as there are more buyers than sellers in a stock it cannot go down and is said to be under *buying pressure*.

Call or call option.   A contract giving the holder the right to buy a stock (usually 100 shares) at a fixed or striking price for a specified length of time.

Capitalization.   For our purposes, the total number of common shares that have been issued and are outstanding for a corporation. The number of shares closely held or unlikely to be available for active trading should be considered. (See Floating supply.)

Cash value.   See Intrinsic value.

Closing purchase transaction.   A call option seller, who has a covered or naked position in an option, terminates his obligation to deliver the stock, should the option be exercised, by *purchasing* an option having the same striking price and expiration date as the option he previously sold. (Or, in the case of a seller of a put, he covers in the same manner to terminate his obligation to take delivery of the stock.)

Closing sale transaction.   The holder of an option liquidates his position by selling an option having the same striking price and expiration date as the option he previously purchased.

Contrary opinion.   The theory that one should take the *opposite* side of whatever the majority, or the public at large, is presently doing. Since the majority usually proves to be wrong, or is the most enthusiastic just when the market is about to fall, the contrary opinion advocate does the opposite of what the majority is doing.

Covered call writer.   One who owns the underlying stock and writes (sells) calls against his stock position.

Covered put writer.   One who is short the underlying stock and writes (sells) puts against his short position.

Cycle.   An undulating, wavelike movement that is periodic in nature. A sine wave would be an example of a perfect cycle, from valley to peak, then back to the valley starting point.

Distribution.   When there are more sellers than buyers in a stock it is said to be under *distribution*. Distribution can be going on in a stock in the early stages of a market top without it being apparent in the stock's price. As selling pressure increases, distribution moves the stock price downward.

Exercise price.   The agreed-to price at which a call buyer can purchase the underlying stock during the life of the call, or sell the stock during the life of a put, also called the "striking price." In the case of a put, the exercise price is the price at which the buyer of the put can "put" the stock to the seller.

Expiration date.   The date that ends the option period. For options on listed exchanges, this is currently the third Friday of the month for the month written.

Floating supply.   The number of common shares available for trading that are not closely held.

Future time value.   That part of an option's price that is greater than its intrinsic, or cash value. This is the part of an option cost one pays for controlling the stock during a specific future time period. It diminishes, or shrinks, as the option period shortens. Often referred to as "the premium" (over intrinsic value).

Gap.   When a stock opens at a higher (or lower) price than it traded the previous day, a gap or space appears on the bar chart where no trading action took place.

In-the-money.   When a call option has intrinsic value because the stock's current market price is above the striking price of the option, it is said to be *in-the-money*. In the case of a put, the stock's current price would have to be *below* the striking price of the option to be termed in-the-money.

Intrinsic value.   The portion of an option's price that represents the cash value of the option, or the amount above the striking price for which the stock is currently selling. For example, if a stock is presently priced at $34 and there is a $30 call available, the intrinsic, or cash value of the call is $4. For a put, the intrinsic value is that amount of the stock's price *below* the striking price.

Leverage.   In this book, the use of a small amount of money for an option contract having the potential for realizing a profit many times the amount originally invested but, at the same time, carrying the risk of total loss of capital. The more leveraged a position is, the greater the risk/reward potential.

Momentum.   The rate of acceleration in expansion of price and volume. This is a key measurement in overall market or individual stock movement.

Moving Balance Indicator (MBI).   A short-term market oscillator devised by Humphrey Lloyd which helps to determine when the market is overbought or oversold.

Naked call option writer.   One who sells or writes a call option without owning the underlying security to support the call position. If the option is exercised, he must buy the underlying stock at the market to fulfill the contract.

Naked put option writer.   One who sells or writes a put without having a short position in the underlying stock. If the option is exercised, the put writer is obligated to buy the stock from the put buyer at the exercise price (regardless of the current market price).

Open interest.   The total number of option contracts in a given option that are outstanding at the present time.

Out-of-the-money.   When a call option has no intrinsic value because the stock's current price is less than the striking price, it is said to be *out-of-the-money*. In the case of a put, the stock's current price would be *above* the striking price to be termed out-of-the-money.

Oscillator.   An indicator that moves cyclically from one extreme to the other, tipping and changing direction much as a see-saw does.

Overbought.   The condition in the market, or individual stock, suggesting that there are no more buyers to fuel a rally and that a reversal in trend is imminent.

Oversold.   The condition in the market or individual stock, suggesting that there are no more sellers to lower prices and that a reversal in trend is imminent.

Parity.   An option is said to have reached parity when the exercise price plus the time premium is equal to the current price of the underlying stock. Once an option reaches parity, the option price tends to move point for point with the underlying stock.

Premium.   The amount an option buyer pays for a contract. Used by some to designate the time value, or that portion of the total option price that is not intrinsic value.

Put or put option.   An option giving the owner a right to sell (usually 100 shares) the underlying stock at a fixed price for a stated period of time.

Selling pressure.   As long as there are more sellers than buyers in a stock, it cannot go up, and is said to be under selling pressure.

Speculator.   One who is willing to assume a great deal of risk in the hope of receiving greater than usual gains. A speculator is looking for high leverage and large capital gains rather than slow appreciation and safe return.

Strike or striking price.   The price at which an option may be exercised. Put and call options are quoted by expiration date and striking price, for example, "Jan. 40."

Strong hands.   The smart money, the insiders and professional people in the security industry, who usually know what they are doing. They buy low and sell high—to weak hands.

Summation principle.   The concept that a number of cycles of varying time periods are at work in a stock (or market average) at the same time. The sum of these (or summation) accounts for the variations in length, magnitude and velocity of market moves.

Technical indicators.   As applied to the stock market, technical indicators are tools used by analysts to predict future trends. They are based on past time/data relationships such as stock prices, market and economic statistics.

Technical rebound.   A short, reflex rally in a downtrend, sometimes also referred to as a *bounce*.

Trader's Index.   A market indicator based on a ratio of advancing issues/declining issues divided by advancing volume/declining volume. It can be found on Bunker Ramo machines by punching MKDS.

Weak hands.   The average investor, acting on fundamental information: news stories, broker's suggestions, friends' advice. He is usually *wrong*, buying near the top, holding while a stock goes down, panicking and selling near the bottom. He buys high, sells low—to strong hands.

Volatility.   A measurement of the sensitivity of a stock as it moves in relation to supply and demand. For example, a "thin" or low capitalization stock will move a much greater percentage with a volume increase than highly capitalized stock will. A very popular stock that has caught the public's fancy and has been trading very actively will be more volatile than a staid blue chip that is not in vogue.

Selected Bibliography

Ansbacher, Max G., *The New Option Market* (New York: Walker & Co., 1979).

Cleeton, Claude E., *The Art of Independent Investing: A Handbook of Mathematics, Formulas and Technical Tools for Successful Market Analysis and Stock Selection* (Englewood Cliffs, NJ: Prentice-Hall, 1976). Proven concepts and technical tools of varying degrees of sophistication, relying heavily on mathematical explanations.

Davis, Gary A. and M. Allen Jacobson, *Stock Option Strategies,* (Cross Plains, WI: Badger Press, 1976).

Edwards, Robert D. and John Magee, *Technical Analysis of Stock Market Trends* (Springfield, MA: John Magee). This book is the recognized classic on technical stock chart interpretation.

Gastineau, Gary L., *The Stock Options Manual* (New York: McGraw-Hill, 1975).

Granville, Joseph E., *Granville's New Strategy of Daily Stock Maket Timing for Maximum Profit* (Englewood Cliffs, NJ: Prentice-Hall, 1976). A profound work on day-to-day stock market timing based on accumulation/distribution as well as technical market indicators and market psychology.

Hardy, C. Coburn, *Investors Guide to Technical Analysis* (New York: McGraw-Hill, 1978). A good general reference for the beginner explaining how to use and profit by various types of technical analysis.

Hurst, J.M., *The Profit Magic of Stock Transaction Timing* (Englewood Cliffs, NJ: Prentice-Hall, 1971). One of the best books that has been written on cycles in the stock market, and how to time stock movements.

Jiler, William L., *How Charts Can Help You in the Stock Market* (New York: Trendline, Inc., 1972). A basic and easily interpreted book on chart reading, an excellent reference.

Lloyd, Humphrey E.D., M.D., *The Moving Balance System—A New Technique for Stock and Option Trading,* (Brightwater, NY: Windsor Books, 1976). Presents an excellent short-term indicator to measure overbought and oversold conditions and intermediate direction of the overall stock market.

Loeb, Gerald, *The Battle for Investment Survival* (New York: Simon & Schuster, 1965). Timeless investment wisdom and advice, from a fundamental viewpoint.

Sokoloff, Kiril, *The Thinking Investor's Guide to the Stock Market* (New York: McGraw-Hill, 1978). A noted investment advisor and financial writer provides a masterful book for anyone who wants to better understand market psychology. Also gives practical strategies to apply in the market.

Williams, Larry R., *The Secret of Selecting Stocks for Immediate and Substantial Gains* (Carmel Valley, CA: Conceptual Management, 1972). A classic and original work on how to measure accumulation and distribution of stocks to predict price movement.

Selected Technical Services

Chart and Technical Services

Chartcraft, Inc., 1 West Avenue, Larchmont, NY 10538.

Daily Graphs, William O'Neil & Co., P.O. Box 24933, Los Angeles, CA 90024.

Mansfield, R.W., Co., Inc. P.O. Box 1640, Palmdale, CA 93550.

Securities Research Co., 208 Newbury Street, Boston, MA 02116.

Standard & Poor's Trendline, 25 Broadway, New York, NY 10004.

Technical Advisory Services

Bretz-Juncture Recognition, Box 1209, Pompano Beach, FL 33061.

Granville Market Letter, P.O. Box 58, Holly Hill, FL 32017.

Indicator Digest, 451 Grand Avenue, Palisades Park, NJ 07650.

Investors' Intelligence, 2 East Avenue, Larchmont, NY 10602.

The Maratta Advisory, Inc., 1220 Post Road, Fairfield, CT 06430.

Market Logic, 3417 North Federal Highway, Fort Lauderdale, FL 33306.

Professonial Timing Service (Larry Williams), P.O. Box 7483, Missoula, MT 59807.

Zweig Forecast, 747 Third Avenue, New York, NY 10017.

Index